Echoes in Perspective

Essays on Architecture

Echoes in Perspective

Essays on Architecture

Daniel Pavlovits

BOOKS

Winchester, UK
Washington, USA

First published by iff Books, 2015
iff Books is an imprint of John Hunt Publishing Ltd., Laurel House, Station Approach,
Alresford, Hants, SO24 9JH, UK
office1@jhpbooks.net
www.johnhuntpublishing.com
www.iff-books.com

For distributor details and how to order please visit the 'Ordering' section on our website.

Text copyright: Daniel Pavlovits 2014

ISBN: 978 1 78279 963 4
Library of Congress Control Number: 2014956322

A CIP catalogue record for this book is available from the British Library.

Design: Stuart Davies

Printed in the USA by Edwards Brothers Malloy

We operate a distinctive and ethical publishing philosophy in all
areas of our business, from our global network of authors to
production and worldwide distribution.

CONTENTS

For Mark Cousins, a friend and mentor

Preface

Perspectives on the Architectural

The essays presented here represent close to twelve years of thinking on the margins of architecture after an initial undergraduate education in the discipline. The essays that follow were born out of a two-fold consideration: the first to further an intellectual engagement with the act of architecture from the bowels of my own interests in the discipline, whilst the second was a means to demonstrate an ongoing commitment to architecture by way of honestly thinking through the architectural.

Architects are too often trained in the *métier* of architecture as a commercial outcome, which is evident in many schools of architecture. In doing so, much creativity and joy of discovery and speculation are lost, which consequently comes to bear on the quality, nature and type of architecture that is subsequently produced. As Adam Ferguson in the eighteenth century stated, "The commercial and lucrative arts may continue to prosper, but they gain an ascendant at the expense of other pursuits. The desire of profit stifles the love of perfection. Interest cools the imagination, and hardens the heart"[1] – such is the fate of much architectural production and architectural pursuits in our own time as well, without a wholehearted interest in the speculative and possibility of the creative.

So often, architecture as a discipline and later professional pursuit is confined to the commercial dictates of profit in servitude to lucrative outcomes, in contra-distinction to the possibility of dreaming-up new worlds. The ability to speculate, interrogate, question and thus dream-up new worlds and possibilities is arguably at the heart of what architecture as a discipline should encompass. It was on an Occupy Wall Street banner in 2011 where I read the inspiring words, "Occupy your Heart /

Another World is Possible / Make Ready your Dreams"; it is in such vein that I attempted a pursuit of architecture, of which the following essays are the result.

One could read the collection of essays herein as a political voice to architecture and the architecture profession, constantly gnawing away at the disciplinary, only to find favor in the imaginative, intellectually interesting and the creative. Beyond embodying a collection of thought on architecture and its discipline, the present collection of essays also serves as a not-so-veiled political program for the possibility of architecture, with the aim of re-establishing a desire for architecture as such. If only it were architects doing such thinking, as opposed to writers such as myself, which I have become, the professional class of the discipline might realize something about architecture that goes beyond a mere servitude to the King of profit and its dictates.

Some of the essays presented in this volume may seem to address the topic of architecture and architectural making from left-of-field. However, I see this as justified, as there can be no stricture on an approach to thinking the architectural if it is truly to be called architecture.

The collection begins with a musing on the archaic origins of architecture, which arguably are found in the requirement for shelter and envelopment in response to the dictates and needs of sleep. Following is an essay on the discipline and on the architectural process, the concerns of which are interlinked, in the making of architecture. An essay follows on the question of the repetition of the form-function urtypology derivative of the practice of *Parkour* and how it destabilizes such architectural repetition. After this essay three pieces follow on architecture and politics, the first from the perspective of the meaning of politics for the ancient Greeks, the second on architecture as a possibility for political activism, the third on the politics of digital architecture, or what it should be. The collection continues with seven further essays variably on the possibility of infolding philosophy and the practice of architecture in the pursuit of Peter Eisenman's collaboration with Jacques Derrida, a philosophical musing on the essence of making place, an essay critique of the redevelopment efforts of Ground Zero, the role and possibility of architecture theory, a discussion of the question concerning *poiesis* in architecture, the significance of corners, and a rumination on the meaning of ruins and with it the fate of all architecture.

The title of this volume was chosen as *Echoes in Perspective*, which was taken from one of the late-John Hejduk's poems titled "La Roche" published in his poem anthology *Such Places as Memory*. John Hejduk himself, as an architectural educator and long-standing academic at the Cooper Union for the Advancement of the Arts, was one of those few people in the profession of architecture who championed the creative over the profitable, the imaginative over the intellectually moribund. It is apt, therefore, to take a line from one of his poems that seems to sum-up the act of writing in this collection, as well as that of writing in general in relation to architecture: firstly that the concern of the architectural is found within the meaning and accomplishment of the term "perspective", whilst the writing that confronts it and addresses it might be seen as the sounding of "echoes" forming off such perspectival walls, only to return thinking on the discipline to the profession as a ghost. Such echoes require a voicing as well as perspectival matter off which to refract; therefore the written word is as applicable as anything else in pursuing architectural thinking in the course of pursuing and realizing its perspectives, with indeed the two going hand-in-hand.

Some in the profession are of the position that architects should build, make, design and accomplish function, while the speculative and the interrogative should be left to academics and writers or, more precisely, theorists on architecture. I believe conversely, that architecture can't truly be realized without the speculative and the interrogative, and that both facets require to be folded into one another in order for architecture to truly be pursued. Hence the art of thinking the architectural through in an honest, interesting and important way is as much a part and should be as much a part of disciplinary competence as anything else.

The thus presented essays in this volume are aimed to serve as echoes of thought off the inanimate and the concrete, hoping to infuse making with reflection and inspiration for a possibility of otherness, and to stimulate its readers in the possibility of dreaming-up other worlds. In the least, I hope the current collection of essays will serve as an interesting footnote to the thinking through and consequent making of architecture and its joys, which should include an affordance for speculation and interrogation with rigor. I hope this present collection of essays does justice to both the object of its gaze, which is the architectural, as well as the inspiration to that gaze, the speculative and the intellectual in relation to it.

Daniel Pavlovits
London, March 2014

On the Archaic Origins of Architecture

Watching late-night television one evening starring Tom Hanks in the epic movie *Cast Away*, the story of an ill-fated courier pilot being washed-up on a deserted South Pacific island after his airplane crashed into the ocean and his attempts at survival on the island and escape from it back to civilization, a striking thing was portrayed about the elemental nature of the human condition vis-à-vis envelopment and shelter. This led me to begin to think about the archaic conditions governing the psychological and anthropological genesis of what has become known as architecture in human history, and its fundamental relation to the biological condition.

In the movie *Cast Away*, after being washed-up on this fictional desert island, the protagonist attempts an ill-fated escape back to civilization by attempting to float through the breakers a rubber dingy salvaged from the plane crash. The scene ends in disaster when the rubber dingy is washed back by the waves onto coral, puncturing its fabric. No longer of any use as a floatation device for the purposes of survival at sea, or indeed escape from the desert island, the fabric-hull of the thus ruined rubber dingy is trans-morphed in the scene following into an ad-hoc canopy of shelter for our protagonist in his moment of ordeal.

What struck me in this sequence of scenes, is that despite the constantly balmy and tropical climate in which this desert island is fictionally located, and despite the ample tree-covering of the ground for use as shade from the sun and protection from rain, the protagonist nonetheless found an urge, need and desire that cannot but be construed as archaic, to seek-out and erect a device for shelter, which in any logical analysis, was of no apparent need. What struck me from the portrayal of this scene, is that this act of creating shelter seemed as some sort of archaic and deep-seated psychological and anthropological – even evolutionary –

connection of biological specimens to the need for envelopment.

As we well know, many species, let alone humans, construct for themselves and their offspring, various forms of shelter serving the purpose of envelopment, be it burrows in the ground, nests in trees, nests in streams or rocky outcrops or, as humans did originally, find settlement in caves or other naturally occurring places of shelter. What is unique about this practice is not only the obvious reason to provide shelter from predators and/or elements of nature for the purposes of survival, but it seems as though it might be appropriate to speculate that there exists an archaic, possibly genetic need and desire based within our biology, for a form and type of envelopment – even in apparently idyllic climates such as a tropical desert island.

Thinking about this speculation and reflecting on biology and species of varying intelligence evolved from it, it cannot but raise the question of whether this archaic condition latent within our evolutionary past and psychology leading to anthropology is as such the archaic origins of architecture, for it is arguably within this archaic origin that we find the genesis of what we now practice and understand as architecture.

Of course, the practice of what we consider and recognize as architecture is a development beyond the basic seeking of shelter, specifically marked by the emergence of building and construction of artifices in an artful way – something that is denoted by the Greek term *tékhnē*; its origins might nonetheless arguably be rooted in an archaic psychological and anthropological need and desire for envelopment, something that is present in varied biological species, both animal and plant life beyond the human being. This is to say, that the metaphysics of architecture might be found within a psychological and anthropological distant past rooted in evolution, of which architecture as we know it, with the application of art, artifice and the concept of *tékhnē* to the act of building, is merely an extension.

It would be interesting to study, look into more deeply, and theorize this archaic origin of architecture. No doubt, evolutionary science relating to plant and animal life, anthropological research into indigenous forms of the prehistoric practice of shelter, and not least psycho-analytical sources, including Freud's many case studies, would need to be researched in order to do so. It would also be interesting to speculate and research the effects of an absence of envelopment on psychological wellbeing. In doing so, it might be possible to assert that architecture as we understand it from our civilized human history is none other than a biological condition rooted within evolutionary history, imprinting itself on our psychological past and present. I would give this theoretical study a preliminary title of "The Archaic Origins of Architecture", a study and consequential theorization of the need and desire for envelopment as a fundamental trait of the biological condition and, as an extension, the human condition.

Perhaps it is from within this archaic origin for the need of envelopment that we can argue the development in humankind of building practices in their most rudimentary form – just like our cast-away's practice in the late-night television movie – in addition to beginning to theorize the development of sedentary settlement that arises from it, even the emergence and development of archaic urban forms in early human civilization. Of course anthropology asserts to already possess a theory as to why settlement occurred in early human history, and the reason behind the rise of proto-typical villages and community. However, none of them to my knowledge begin with an evolutionary, biological and psychological reasoning and argument come theory. To do so would be to go beyond the physical archaeological and anthropological study of the practice of prehistoric life, in order to delve into the philosophical, metaphysical and theoretical origins of architecture, of which it might be asserted, that a central component is the archaic desire, urge and need for envelopment as a phenomena and practice, possibly arising from the most basic of biological conditions, the need for sheltered sleep.

Turning our gaze to recent modern practice of architecture and planning, perhaps the reason behind the failure of Modern, twentieth century urban planning might just be able to be explained from such a philosophical study. The fact that Modern architecture and urban planning treated material structure and construction as an object placed within a *carte-blanche* field similar to and extending from Le Corbusier's Plan Voisin project for Paris from 1925, explains why such vision for our urban environment has arguably resulted in failure. The reason arguably being, that it fails to provide and resolve the archaic biological, evolutionary, anthropological and psychological need for an experience and sense of envelopment (beyond the need for shelter) that might do justice to the human condition, instead treating architecture as a series of objects placed within a blank field.

Of course this practice of Modernism in urban planning evolved from a utopian resolution to the disease and decay fostered by historical urbanism; however, a study as such proposed above, might be able to argue its failure from a unique philosophical angle, as opposed to the merely subjective and technologically aesthetic.

There seems something fundamental in the need and desire for envelopment, to which architecture is but a calling. If architecture and urbanism would be understood as a response to an archaic evolutionary, anthropological and psychological need rooted within the biological and psychological human condition, our understanding and indeed development of architectural thinking would alter. This is to say that our subjectivity by which we perceive the utility of architecture would morph from an exercise perhaps in pure development and expenditure of capital for the purposes of return, or even a simplistic practice of aesthetic taste, toward beginning to seek out and address the psychological and evolutionary need in us, and reflecting it and the most basic trait of the human condition back to the world through what might be conceived architecturally.

Some architects indeed already practice this thinking and observation in their own built projects. For instance architecture that seeks to mimic and extend the condition of the traditional macro built environment on a micro-scale is but one example, treating the configuration of an individual building along the lines of a miniature city, creating room and openings for rest and reflection, contrasted with adjacent spaces leading to a prescribed end of uniqueness or destination, possibly connected through a vista of sorts either visual or audible, in the same manner that nineteenth century urban planning envisioned the layout of the city in places such as Paris (but of course for other reasons), or to a lesser extent some parts of London. This, of course, is not to make an argument for the return of such nineteenth century form in the present day, but rather to comprehend something about the principle of envelopment as central to the concern and psychological wellbeing of human beings and their experience of an environment, albeit practiced and achieved in a contemporary, critical, and even radical way. Criticality always emerges from theory, from a deep understanding of an issue, and what such a study and theory of envelopment might offer as the one being ruminated on here, is insight into new ways toward contemporary criticality in practice.

Herein lies the possibility of architecture and the thinking through of architectural possibilities toward the realization of envelopment as one of the most basic and fundamental urges within the human condition. Such thinking lays out the possibility to rethink the practice and articulation of architecture in a way that transcends itself and begins to speak to our innermost needs, thoughts, feelings and desires as latent within an ur-psychogeography. At the point of this latent ur-psychogeography coming into practice, we would experience architecture as an immanence and extension of everything that makes us who we are, reflecting back to us in turn our most basic psychological needs and desires that have perhaps long since been forgotten, merely to be reawakened from the depths of our unconscious.

Architecture based on such a premise, research and practice might be the beginnings of a new subjectivity in architecture, a subjectivity that might just result in doing justice to an archaic evolutionary, biological, anthropological and psychological source, need and desire, resolving in its wake everything from form through to function, and arresting and then suspending the way we experience, feel and think of ourselves in, and as a result of, architecture and the urban condition: envelopment, where desire may live.

The Discipline of Architecture and the Architectural Process

In asking the question of what entails the act of architecture, the initial question that must be asked is, what is it that composes the discipline of architecture? The fact that the act of architecture akin to other professional pursuits is born of an education relating to a specific knowledge base, and is bounded by such knowledge base, makes it obviously a procedure that is disciplinary in nature. Setting out the boundaries of knowledge and craft related to the act of architecture is initially none other than setting out the boundaries of the discipline of architecture.

In beginning to answer the question of the boundaries of the discipline of architecture, a crucial starting consideration might be the nature, meaning and etymological origin of the term "discipline". The modern English term "discipline" arises in our language from the Old French term *descepline*, which in turn arises from the Latin *disciplīna*, meaning to impart instruction to a disciple who is being initiated into a practice. The English term disciple arises from the Latin *discipulus* meaning a pupil, which person is in a position of receiving instruction in a certain activity or craft. The term of *discipulus* is formed from the lost compound of *discipere*, meaning to grasp intellectually or analyze thoroughly, creating the Medieval Latin term *disciplinare* from around 1300, meaning to chastise, related to the Latin *disciplīna* meaning instruction.[1]

Thus the discipline of architecture and the consequent act of making architecture rests and resides partially within receiving instruction and "chastisement" in the form of a pupil from people who practice the discipline, in order to gain knowledge and intellectual insight into the act of architecture, and furthermore to be able to analyze thoroughly that which pertains to the making of architecture. Thus the cradle of the discipline of architecture is its many and varied schools of architecture where instruction, learning and a passing on of knowledge occur for the purposes of (re)creating that which is architectural or could be deemed as architecture, resulting in the architectural act.

The basis of such education, knowledge and learning in relation to the discipline of architecture, which still holds true today, was articulated by Vitruvius in his *De architectura* (*Ten Books on Architecture*) in the 1ˢᵗ century BCE, in which central to all architecture are the three qualities of *firmitas, utilitas, venustas* – translating to that which is solid, useful and beautiful. Thus the core competency of a person within the discipline of architecture must be to produce structures which are solid – not prone to falling down or collapsing; useful – that is satisfy the needs and requirements of their users; and beautiful – that is satisfy an aesthetic category that has changed and continues to change over the course of the centuries, but which can nonetheless be recognized in something that is executed.

The discipline of architecture and the very act of making, conceiving and drawing up a building, space or series of buildings that might be conceived as an act of architecture, is predicated upon the instruction and knowledge gained during an education in its discipline, and is a kind of built structure that satisfies all the requirements of its users in a way that is solid in its construction, useful to its intended users, whilst furthermore aesthetically interesting, contributive or suitable to the location in which it is set.

In the modern conception of such disciplinary parameters, the discipline and education – and later professional output – of an architect in the course of conceiving architecture thus must resolve the requirements and strictures of various and numerous building codes relating to structural adequacy, fire, water, light, ventilation and insulation, to name just a few parameters, whilst achieving this in a materiality that satisfies the needs of the users who will come to use the building, and do so in an aesthetically interesting, pleasing or suitable way in relation to its context, making it thus beautiful.

Further to the above minimum disciplinary competency relating to the modern act of architecture, architectural education and later professional delivery, the modern discipline of architecture requires all of the above to be realized in a way that is cost-effective and within a certain budget of the builder or commissioner, realizing a profit for the thus mentioned developer. The discipline of architecture thus educates and instructs the pupil of architecture to a level of competency in which the outcome of his ideas and solutions to problems given the eventual users of his building and the site in which it is located, satisfy the building codes, create something suitable in terms of function, produce something that is pleasing aesthetically, and additionally fall within the budget of the investment.

In setting out to demonstrate such competency in the discipline of architecture across various scales and intended uses of building, a judicious choice and realization of structural systems, related materials, type and limitation of construction cost and time must all be paid heed to. Furthermore, all of this must be executed and achieved in a way that satisfies all of the needs of the buildings' users pertaining to solutions for light, ventilation, energy use, comfort and circulation, and do so in an aesthetically pleasing or interesting way.

In the discipline of architecture in which a pupil might engage, disciplining processes are at play in the course of training and education of an architect along the parameters of the above limits. The disciplining processes entail in addition to the sum of the above, a competency in the use of drawing, calculating and the use of visualization aids, be it models, computer drawings or animation, for the purpose of being able to fulfill a competent role within the industry of the profession of architecture within an architecture firm, studio or as a sole trader.

It must be noted that the above requirements of the discipline of architecture resulting in an ability to act as an architect are barely the sole minimum of the potential and promise of architecture as a discipline. Although the sum of the above capacities and competencies might qualify a person thus educated to become a member of the architecture profession in whatever jurisdiction and thus call himself or herself an "architect", the true art of architecture is something that goes way beyond a basic competency of the discipline thus far recognized.

Throughout the centuries, arising from around the fifteenth century in which Leon Battista Alberti wrote his *De Re Aedificatoria (On the Art of Building)*, architecture has increasingly become disciplined, codified, and bounded in various ways both socially, economically, politically, institutionally and professionally. Yet, despite its multi-faceted nature, it is defined in separation from "building" by other areas of expertise and competency both intellectual and academic. These further attributes of the architect are what brings the basic competency of being able to conceive, visualize and execute a building into a higher realm that begins to satisfy cultural and intellectual considerations of his/her time, culture and context. This later competency is perhaps not so much disciplinary in relation to the professional competency of the architect, but intellectual in his/her competency of the architectural process. Such process goes beyond the mere minimum competency of achieving something that is solid, useful and beautiful, and begins to enter upon a set of cultural and intellectual parameters, which thus embraced involve a willed effort of intellectual extrapolation and understanding in relation to civilizational cues. It is in this competency that the architectural process, as opposed to the disciplinary process of education in architecture, is realized.

The discipline and disciplining of a pupil in the act of creating architecture in the course and result of an architectural education and the eventual becoming part of the architecture profession contributes to disciplining the subject in a particular way. This disciplining is not the same as the ability to think creatively and be able to "read" culture and civilizational cues as a starting point for making something of material construction that on the one hand satisfies, and on the other goes beyond making something that is solid, useful and beautiful. Indeed, it might be argued that the disciplining process of a lot of architecture schools and of the modern architecture profession imbues precisely the opposite outcome to creativity, inquiry and speculation that the architectural process requires.

The disciplining nature of an architectural education and resultant basic professional competency so often comes to act as a limit to possibilities and creativity, as opposed to a starting point for it, and this because a disciplinary process involves power and authority; challenging or attempting to go beyond such authoritative structure and stricture often draws resistance to it, precisely because of the mechanisms of power and authority built into the disciplinary structure.

The British author Iain Sinclair has written that, "Human thought is crush'd beneath the iron hand of Power"[2], and such is the case when a pupil who by definition in the disciplinary process is subject to power, begins or desires to want to go beyond the mere dictates of disciplinary competence for the purposes of beginning to engage honestly and truthfully a journey into the architectural process. Indeed, the disciplinary process as an authority and power in the education of pupils in the basic competency of the act of architecture can often not act otherwise but in a delimiting way toward a desire for the architectural process.

It was Herbert Marcuse of the Frankfurt School in 1936, who wrote in his *A Study on Authority*, that:

The recognition of authority as a basic force of social praxis attacks the very roots of human freedom: it means (in a different sense in each case) the surrender of autonomy (of thought, will, action) the tying of the subjects' reason and will to pre-establish contents, in such a way...[that they] are taken over as they stand as the obligatory norms for his reason and will[3].

So often, such is the case of disciplinary procedures and limits in relation to the possibility of the architectural process. When a pupil wants to enter upon the architectural process in relation to civilizational and cultural parameters, and intellectually engage his/her making something solid, useful and beautiful with considerations that go beyond the strictly speaking solid, useful and beautiful, only to reveal something in turn in the subject of the user that might be edifying beyond mere use or an aesthetically pleasing value-judgment, a limit of disciplining authority so often prevails.

Disciplinary competency of architecture on the one hand, and the process of architecture on the other are not strictly speaking one and the same thing. The efficacy of the authority of architectural disciplining is not the same as the ability to enter into the architectural process. Disciplinary competency and education often delimit the freedom of exploration desired by a pupil in being able to enter terrains intellectual that might inform his/her making of architecture in a different and even unique, interesting and important way, if for no other reason than the limited amount and period of time given to realize a project within an educational setting that might be available before the project is to be evaluated against the parameters of competency. Thus in returning to the words of Herbert Marcuse, "the concept of authority [...] leads back to the concept of freedom: it is the practical freedom of the individual, his social freedom and its absence, which is at stake"[4].

By the "architectural process", what is meant is everything that precedes the act of drawing and realizing something built that is competently executed according to disciplinary requirements. What is meant by the architectural process is the world of thought and inquiry that goes into informing how and why something should be built or realized in a certain way, and to what end. What is meant by the architectural process is an engagement with the entire "life-world" of the human for the purposes of exploring and then realizing in built form new thoughts, the creation of new feelings, a realization of subjective alterity and a renewal of spatial intervention and spatial reading by the users in the course of inhabiting and occupying a building or space along a set of lines intellectually formed and argued for. Such outcome can only be realized if the source of such experimentation and inquiry comes from the outside of the professional boundaries of architecture, that is from the broader humanities or sciences, which when brought into the architectural process realizes architecture that is unique, interesting and important. Such inquiry and intellectual curiosity into the origin of the thought process of making architecture is a prerequisite condition of being able to realize architecture as such, and is also something that lies outside disciplinary competency strictly speaking. We might say that the architectural process is everything before and beyond the point when one reaches disciplinary competency, and for which disciplinary competency is the means to be able to execute it.

No doubt, architecture is conditioned by an urtypology that endlessly and ceaselessly is beheld to repetition of form and function as Andrew Benjamin has analyzed the possibility of architecture in his *Architectural Philosophy*[5], which in turn the disciplinary nature of education champions. This is to say that a staircase requires certain parameters of function that couple with a repetition of its form, as do in most cases walls and other functional elements, which become disciplinary parameters of making something solid, useful and beautiful without any thought of inquiry into how they might be able to be executed otherwise, and for what reason. The question, however, in relation to the architectural process is precisely this: how might the form of the staircase, wall, partition, roof, window or structural member be construed in a way that still satisfies its purposed function, which is to say utility or usefulness, but does so in a way that changes the users' perception of it and the rest of the space and how it works and is organized, only to reveal something beyond the mere disciplinary competency of making architecture. Such consideration arises from everything that precedes competency in being able to realize something solid, useful and beautiful. Such consideration requires an intellectual curiosity and inquiry into making something that speaks to the user or users, without forgoing the urtypoligical condition of repetition that the architectural form-function relationship is beholden to. Entering upon such an architectural process exists in precisely circumventing disciplinary authority in competent spatial production in thinking through and realizing a built environment, leading to what might be termed a critical exploration of the possibilities of architecture, producing in the users something beyond the satisfaction of mere utility.

The possibility and promise of the architectural process resides in producing an opening for alterity in thought, whilst satisfying the dictates of competency in relation to function. Because the urtypology of architecture between function and form is based upon a repetition of the same, a different way of conceiving spatial or surface execution creates subjective alterity in the user, precisely because it upsets this relationship. It is in entering this process, which is none other than the architectural process in the actuality of producing a particular piece of architecture, that architecture as such is born. It is in this ability that competence should need to be demonstrated in order for architecture to follow, and that in the vein of the disciplinary requirements of firmness, utility and beauty.

The question which resides at the heart of the architectural process and inquiry is therefore, how can new thoughts and new feelings emerge as a result of a particular way of resolving function and form; how can one create subjective alterity in the users of the space; how can one inject civilizational and cultural parameters of thought into the making of a piece of architecture? If competency in architectural production is merely beholden to the guiding authority of disciplinary measures alone as outlined above, nothing new, interesting or important will ever surface in architecture, precisely because of the relationship between form and function as an architectural urtypology being beholden to repetition. The architectural process thus starts prior to and reaches beyond disciplinary competency, and strives to question the very nature and condition of space and its subjective content that it might throw upon the user. Such is the process of criticality, invention and alterity in architectural conception.

In logically following through the previous remarks in relation to the efficacy of the architectural process, the question must be posed, "What would happen if the question of repetition and that of function were to be destabilized in architecture?" The answer to this question is that an alterity would enter the subjective space (thoughts and feelings) of the user of such architecture that would shift the resultant space toward the enacting of otherness, at least as far as that otherness remains fit for use. If the destabilization of the form-function relationship goes far enough to completely separate one from the other, sculpture ensues. Whilst other ways of executing and realizing the repetition of the relation between function and form remain within the realm of their intended utility – that is their relationship is only partially destabilized – the realization of the space as such would then become an intellectual interrogation and resolution of whatever cultural, scientific or civilizational parameters the architectural process is working through, and at the same time a negation and a critique of architecture as such, whilst still remaining within the boundaries of disciplinary competency as such.

What then is the potential efficacy and role of the architectural process in the built environment, whilst maintaining a competency in firmness, utility and beauty? How might the built environment alter if an increasing tendency arose to undermine the disciplinary authority of repetition of function/form in architecture toward the creation of different ways of realizing the inherent repetition contained in function relating to form? The answer to this is that architecture would result in such a way that begets the creation of subjective alterity in the users, which is nothing other than the opening up of the users' experience of the space onto new terrains, enabling new thoughts and new feelings to emerge, which arguably lies at the heart of realizing architecture and embarking on the architectural process, be it through intended "sculptural follies" that don't provide any utility, or through intended other ways of realizing function that does.

Examples of such architecture that have entered upon the architectural process whilst remaining within – but at the same time destabilizing – the urtypological relationship between function and form within their context abound. For the sake of brevity, three examples will be discussed below, whilst a fourth also will be mentioned that completely moves beyond and breaks down the repetitive nature of the relationship between function and form.

The first example of such architecture, many examples of which we could mention, might be the Pompidou Center in Paris, which realizes its circulation, structural and ventilation/waste systems in a way diametrically opposed to its context. In the historically traditional architecture that surrounds the Pompidou Center, the circulation within buildings, their structural systems, as well as their systems of waste management lie hidden behind the facades of the buildings. In the Pompidou Center's architectural conception and execution, this relationship is reversed, whereby the function and the building's elements and the eventual form of the building produced by it become destabilized in relation to norms of its context and traditional ways of relating the two to each other.

Another example of architecture in which such architectural process is evident might be the Daniel Libeskind designed Jewish Museum in Berlin, whereby the psychology of entrapment, escape, death and flight, which have historically marked the Jewish experience in Europe and in Germany in particular during the nineteenth and twentieth centuries, inform the experience of circulation within the building and in relation to its exhibits. What is achieved by way of such process of architectural conception in this piece of architecture is an experiential envelopment of the historical Central European Jewish experience in its users through a particular form-function interrelationship, thus imbuing the users of the building with some of the psychological experiences and history of Jews in Central Europe through the very way the architecture of the building and its related exhibit space has been thought through and conceived.

A third example might be Le Corbusier's Villa Savoye, which plays on newfound twentieth century construction technologies in architecture to create a certain structural resolution to the building, which informs the form of the building from its entrance, through to its circulation pattern and openings and related spaces, attempting to create an example of a "machine for living" that might mimic, convey and resolve the machinic condition of modern industry and production.

In all three above examples, the function-form relationship of repetition according to an urtypology is maintained, albeit partially to varying degrees and in different ways destabilized, for the purposes of opening up new readings and new experiences of space in their respective resolution, each according to their respective process of thought, which is the mark and resolution of their architectural process in realizing something architectural, and their architectural act. The fourth example worth mentioning goes completely beyond the possibility of the form-function urtypological relationship, resulting in an almost complete destabilization and breakdown of utility. This project is Bernard Tschumi's 1982-87 "follies" project for Parc de la Villette in Paris.

In Bernard Tschumi's Parc de la Villette project, a series of red steel mostly geometrically perpendicular structures in both internal structure and relation to each other come to mark out the area of the park. The structures are realized, however, in no relationship to possible real utility, neither in their structure completely, nor in their relationship to each other within the park, or to the park itself. Thus the structures become "follies" in which maybe solidity and beauty are realized, but without recourse to utility. By realizing form without recourse to utility, the architectural structures completely destabilize the relationship required between form and function within the prescribed framework of inter-related resolution of *firmitas, utilitas, venustas*. Nonetheless, this is intentionally so, as a means to deconstruct architectural truth and function, and because of this the buildings come to act as a critique on architecture according to a particular architectural process of thought in the process of realizing what was to be built and how, merely one whose result lies beyond conventional measures of architectural utility.

In all four examples of architecture mentioned, conscious architectural processes are at play which have been informed by intellectual and creative curiosity that have come to inform the realized structures – whether satisfying utility or not. Such intellectual processes are what mark the resultant architecture as going beyond mere disciplinary competency to become acts of architecture as such. Acts of architecture thus require an intellectual engagement with issues civilizational, cultural or even mere architectural in order to inform a realization of structure, form and function resulting in architecture. It is this which is termed as the architectural process.

The architectural process can depart from and engage any area of human knowledge; it might arise from and extrapolate aspects of the sciences, it might arise from and extrapolate aspects of the humanities, or it might arise from and extrapolate cultural and/or historic considerations. Arguably, however, what needs to be studied and mastered in relation to realizing an architectural process and a resultant architectural act, is not the strict disciplinary competencies of how to realize something built, but precisely the scientific, the artistic, the philosophical or the cultural reading of cues and their realization in built form. These areas strictly speaking lie outside the basic competency of disciplinary education in architecture; however, the means by which they enter into an architectural process does not; without them the architectural act and the process of thinking up architecture cannot be realized.

The realization of the architectural act therefore requires a broader and deeper engagement with knowledge and learning than might be always and necessarily available in an architectural education setting within a school of architecture in relation to the basic competencies of professional competency. The architectural process resulting in the architectural act involves looking out beyond the narrow focus of disciplinary boundaries in which demonstrated competencies the profession of architecture and its status rests, toward other disciplines such as social theory, aesthetic theory, material theory, the study of movement and of the human subject and a myriad other possible areas of knowledge, and to draw from such study conclusions that might come to enrich human beings by way of what is built.

The only way to realize the architectural process is to glance sideways, and keep on glancing sideways until one truly begins to understand human nature, human desire, human happiness and the way it is structured and assembled, and the things and condition of things through which it is structured and assembled. It is only subsequent to such understanding that an architect can begin to achieve the architectural act, which by definition is always something beyond mere competency in being able to build, visualize, draw and conceive buildings. Anything short of such process remains within the strictures of disciplinary power and authority, holding little lasting cultural, artistic or intellectual legacy. In not doing so, in not glancing sideways and in continuing to not glance sideways onto these human disciplines, the effort of architects and their architecture cannot but result in a form of commercial waste. Architecture by default is a human discipline and a cultural and civilizational discipline that *requires* a thorough study of other areas of knowledge before it can be attempted, which consideration goes beyond mere disciplinary competency. It is this that the architectural process is embodied and assembled by.

Architecture as a field of practice, knowledge and education must by necessity be broad in its scope and range of methods, both practical and theoretical. This is made explicit by Vitruvius when he wrote in *Ten Books on Architecture* that, "the architect should be equipped with knowledge of many branches of study and varied kinds of learning ... knowledge [which] is the child of practice and of theory"[6]. He lists drawing, geometry, history, philosophy, music, medicine, law, astronomy and astrology. Architects and students of architecture still engage with some of these, as well as more recently formed areas of study such as social science, geography, biological sciences, linguistic theory and digital media, and should always do so as a means of informing their architectural process in pursuit of their act of architecture.

The reason an inter-disciplinary and even trans-disciplinary approach is required for the resolution of architecture is that architecture resides within the architectural process, which by definition is inter-disciplinary and even trans-disciplinary. The inter-disciplinary and trans-disciplinary nature of the architectural process is what might be termed as the critical edges, boundaries or essential codes of the discipline. Without such process, nothing productive in architecture beyond building for commercial return can eventuate.

Architecture and the architectural act are critically interdependent with other disciplines and areas of knowledge, and it is in incorporating these areas of knowledge into the formation of thought on space, form and function that lasting, interesting and important architecture can be realized. Architecture is a discipline that emerges from culture and is shaped by it. A thorough engagement and infused inter-disciplinarity in relation to civilization and culture is therefore the pre-requisite of architectural knowledge, of the architectural process and of the architectural act.

Parkour and Architecture

In recent decades a new form of urban exercise and competitive sport has emerged, which bases itself upon the practitioner moving and finding their way through a built environment in a creative self-styled manner, often at speed. The movement is called *Parkour*, which takes its name from the French term *parcours* meaning course.

During the practice of *Parkour*, the practitioner moves through what for them is considered an obstacle course of a built environment such as a housing estate or other urban environment in such a way as to displace normal paths, cues and trajectories of movement. In the practice of *Parkour*, the normal, architecturally and culturally conceived and designed patterns of movement through a built environment become superseded by other, perhaps more efficient, but nonetheless more creative methods of movement and spatial reading. *Parkour* indeed has thus been termed alternatively as *l'art du déplacement*, meaning the art of displacement, whereby the person practicing it, "adopts other ways than those set-out architecturally or culturally"[1] for moving through an environment, and as such displaces the habitual cues of movement through a space.

The emergence of such a sport tells us two things most immediately about architecture: the first, that culturally recognized architectural elements of form such as stairs, doors, railings, parapets, ledges and walkways are forms of repetition that control and prescribe methods of movement, and which people use in a thus pre-determined culturally recognized way; secondly, that other ways of moving through built form is possible, one that results in an art of displacement of the prescribed and dictated mode of use and movement associated with cultural forms and prescribed by them.

From such recognition it follows that architecturally and

culturally recognized forms begetting movement through a space might be considered in some cases to delimit modes of movement, the use and experience of a space. Thus we might say that the culturally and architecturally recognized forms of repetition normally used in the built environment are elements of form that Deleuze and Guattari might term as striated elements of form[2], elements that harness a pre-determined and pre-attached, delimited and delimiting mode of use. Such forms enable and dictate movement in a pre-prescribed manner in their method of use, whereby a door, a parapet, a walkway, a balcony has a certain function attached to it, which function in turn pre-determines and delimits its habitual use.

The art of *Parkour*, however, turns the perception of function of habitual use of such built forms into another reading, one in which their function produces an entirely different pattern of behavior and movement in relation to their form. *Parkour* thus destabilizes the function of such pre-determining elements of form, which if we take them to be striated elements of form predetermining behavior and use, achieves a "deterritorialising" of them, borrowing again a Deleuze/Guattarian term, toward smooth space as an anti-thesis to the pre-determined habitual and thus striated pattern of function they culturally inhabit.

Thus architecture and culturally recognized elements of form within architecture can be put to use in two opposing yet inter-connected ways: one as a culturally recognized norm of form and related function preceding from it, which produces a delimi-tation of use and behavior in relation to it, the other as a recog-nition of possibility for otherness and other movement, use and behavior in relation to such form, producing different modes of movement, use and behavior than culturally might be recog-nized in relation to it. In doing so, *Parkour* enables a deterritori-alising of the striated coupling of form and function toward the smooth inhabitation and movement across a built environment.

What the practice of *Parkour* might reveal to architects is that function and form are not necessarily a stable coupling, and while function-form in some instances might delimit and prescribe behavior, movement, experience and use, it might also in some other instances enable other types of behaviors, movement, experience and use. The challenge therefore that such a recognition might reveal to architects, is that form should not necessarily always be coupled with a pre-determined, culturally habitual function, and if indeed such coupling between form and function is detached in the architect's mind and practice, the possibility for an otherness of use, behavior, movement and experience of the space might be enabled to be had. Indeed for architects to enable an other experience of use, behavior and movement in and through their architecture by users, precisely such a de-coupling of form and function is required, one that results in striated space deterritorialising toward the smooth.

Deleuze and Guattari conceive of smooth and striated space philosophically as, "...nomad space and sedentary space – the space in which the war machine develops and the space instituted by the State apparatus"[3]. The pre-determined, culturally habitual behavior and use of the function-form couple is of the striated nature of space, which is to say of the State apparatus. Such apparatus delimits and codifies the possibility of use and behavior, and thus an experience of a space, and it is for these reasons of codification and delimitation that it is conceptualized as striated. Smooth space on the other hand is conceptualized as the space of the nomad, the space in which the war machine develops, a space in which function and form are decoupled, and an invention by necessity of use and function takes place. Such is the nature of *Parkour's l'art du déplacement* in relation to movement and use, namely the emergence of the possibilities of an other function that such striated, pre-determined and codified form prescribes.

Deleuze and Guattari go on to say about smooth and striated space that:

...no sooner must [we] remind ourselves that the two spaces in fact exist only in mixture: smooth space is constantly being translated, transversed into a striated space [and] striated space is constantly being reversed, returned to a smooth space. In the first case, one organizes even the desert; in the second, the desert gains and grows; and the two can happen simultaneously[4].

Whilst a complete decoupling of form and function in relation to use, movement and experience may be had at an extreme level such as in the art of *Parkour*, this is not necessarily always the only outcome and mode of use and behavior that might follow. What indeed Deleuze and Guattari conceptualize is that the two modes of behavior, movement, experience and use are interconnected, at times deterritorialising toward the smooth, and at other times being reversed and captured by the striated: the two exist in a reciprocal relationship to one another.

Because the smooth and the striated outcomes of experience of form-function elements exist in a reciprocal manner to one another, deterritorialisation mustn't be seen as the sole goal of possible radical use of culturally habitual form. What it does mean, is that in some cases behavior, movement and use might deterritorialise toward other patterns of use, and in other instances it will retain its culturally habitual use. It is in the mixture of these two patterns of perception of use that culturally recognized elements of architecture might be able to perform in a unique reading of space and consequential use. What is paramount for the architect to realize in order to activate both smooth and striated modes of behavior in a built environment is the incorporation of culturally recognized elements of architecture in a not necessarily straightforward reading of use. By doing so, the architect destabilizes and displaces the perception of formal elements within his/her work and opens up the possibility of another reading and another behavior to be activated. In this way, architecture becomes interesting and playful, enabling interesting and playful outcomes of use of space in the manner of play attributable to the architecture of Constant Nieuwenhuys' New Babylon project.

In Constant's New Babylon project, architecture was conceived in a way as to deliberately engender an experience of a different or heterogeneous occupation of space and reciprocally of the urban environment. What Constant wanted to achieve was precisely a foregrounding of the smooth characteristics of space, of enabling different, other and heterogeneous occupation of space as opposed to a mono-mode of occupation and behavior within a given space. Culturally ingrained modes of behavior in relation to the form-function couple produce a mono-mode of behavior in relation to function: only one mode of use is enabled in the perception of the user. New Babylon on the other hand was a project whereby different perceptions of use and consequential behavior in a space might flourish, as a result of a heterogeneous reading of and responding to its elements as a consequence of how they might be read. The New Babylon project of Constant aimed to liberate the relationship between use, form and function for other ways of organizing space and behavior to come to the fore: such is the act of world-making.

In order to be a "world maker", which is to say in order to be able to create different experiences, different sensations, different and other modes of use and behavior, in order for a space to engender a liberation and heterogeneity of occupation, a type of space is required that deliberately enables otherness in its mode of occupation. To do this, architects must consciously enable different readings and consequential different outcomes than culturally might be habitual in and through the resolution of their work, which in turn come to deliberately create unperceived resonances of perception, behavior and related consequences through use. To do so is to go against the grain of making architecture that adheres to culturally registered habitual readings of its elements, which if done, turns architecture on its head, and with it any and all related habitual behavior and patterns of use relating to it.

The seeming reason for the relevance of such deterritoriali-sation of the architectural form-function relationship is that only by introducing difference into culturally accepted habitual modes of use can any otherness of perception emanate from the built environment and from a piece of architecture. Only when the possibility of difference is incorporated into the perception of function and the related form which cues that function, can new thoughts, new feelings and new patterns of behavior and use emerge, which when they do, realize a new and different way of inhabiting and using the space. When new patterns of behavior and use emerge in relation to function, architecture partakes in a process of re-subjectification of the user in relation to their culturally and habitually pre-determined pattern of reading a space and using it and behaving in its midst; it is this process and promise of re-subjectification and playfulness of a space creating new subjectivities that makes a piece of architecture affective and thus produces the possibility for it to become a political agent of potential otherness.

It is arguably precisely otherness that is required in order to make a space or built environment unique and interesting. So much of architecture and the built environment are predicated on the repetition of the form-function urtypological couple, to the point whereby architecture loses its affective capacity. It is precisely a space's effectiveness as an agent for other types of behavior and an otherness of function amidst the myriad spaces of form-function repetition that sets it up as a space of uniqueness and importance. The measure of an urban or otherwise built environment's uniqueness and interestingness is precisely the degree to which it produces otherness in the perception of its users in relation to function.

Deterritorialising striating elements of form-function toward smooth modes of use allows the users of a space to conceive of it and their environment and activity within that environment differently, opening up the perception of function of a space onto new horizons. Such opening up of horizons relating to function onto a new plane allows for a subjective alterity to be realized beyond the necessary beauty and firmness that any built environment may and needs to convey.

Architecture realized along lines that might be interpreted from the practice of *Parkour* as an art of displacement teaches us that architecture, if conceived in a particular way, has the possibility to enable new horizons and new behaviors in relation to function and form to come into existence, which when it does, breaks down the norms and expectations of use, perception, behavior and even structure, opening up the users' experience of the space onto new terrains, terrains which might be populated by different modes of inhabitation in a myriad of unforeseen, interesting and unique ways.

If indeed architects are "world makers", then it is foremost this that we might learn from the art and practice of *Parkour*. Once such space is thought-up and realized, any "normal" expectation of use and related function comes to be suspended, only for each and every person both individually and collectively to realize in that space their own mode of living. Therefore rightly might we say: may heterogeneity and consequential displacement reign, and may form and function be deterritorialised according to an enablement of and generosity toward new behaviors and new types of occupying a space! May architecture enter the realm of world-making, and a particular type of world at that.

Architecture as Politics

Some might suggest that the purpose of architecture is to provide functional shelter for work, living and other daily uses of humans within the context of the capitalist economics of outlay and return, adhering to the dictates of the profit motive. Others might suggest that architecture is an aesthetic pursuit of sorts providing qualitative content and qualitative space to the city. In surmising these suggestions, what could be argued to be the *raison d'etre* of architecture? What is its consequential purpose, and how might it be conceived of as a practice?

Drawing on the thought of Hannah Arendt and her *The Human Condition*, this essay will argue that architecture, like anything else we do, is informed by a political life-world, and that it is first and foremost a political activity. Even if the goal of an architect and her architecture is to create functional space that adheres to the dictates of the profit motive, and/or in addition returns aestheticized space to the city and its users, this motivation and action might be argued to be in itself conditioned by values that might be qualified as political in their very nature. By referring to such activity as political, what is meant are values whose content has come to be shaped by the condition of our age and us in it. If the pursuit of architecture in our age is marked by a refraction of the political-economic value-system of our time, and thus conditioned to perform an outcome, then to what end might architects deploy their action?

Following on from these introductory remarks, and to begin to introduce an extrapolation on the question of how architecture might in its very nature and condition correspond with political action as a means to go beyond the dictates of function, profit and aesthetics, it must first be qualified what the nature of politics is, and an analogy drawn between it and the substantive condition of architecture. In doing so we might turn to Hannah

Arendt's *The Human Condition* to ascertain how the political has been conceived in both our distant and more recent past, and what the relations of its conception might be to the substantive condition of architecture praxis.

Hannah Arendt writes of ancient Greek politics that:

> The root of the ancient estimation of politics [was] the conviction that man *qua* man, each individual in his unique distinctness, appears and confirms himself in speech and action, and that these activities, despite their material futility, possess an enduring quality of their own because they create their own remembrance[1].

Given Arendt's analysis, the ancient practice and conception of the political finds its conduit through the two pillars of speech and action.

Arendt's conception of politics could initially be translated – remaining at first with action – as that whatever produces through action, something that is born from and achieved through the human act, takes on the condition of the political. It is in such initial Arendtian understanding and extrapolation that we enter into the terrain of what the ancient Greeks conceptualized as the nature of politics as far as the component of action is concerned. All and any action for the ancient Greeks found its fulfillment and appearance as a political act: their action became a substantive content of politics as a result of making an appearance, of being performed or executed. The political in this ancient conception is thus tied to appearance, to what appears, to what comes about.

Whatever consequences one might wish to draw from action as one side of the ancient Greek conception and practice of politics, one thing that *can* be drawn is that something by necessity results from it that is seen, something comes about as a consequence to it being conceived and executed, something appears that creates affect. It is this condition of consequence that Aristotle called the *bios politikos*, namely that, "of all the activities necessary and present in human communities, only two were deemed to be political...action (*praxis*) and speech (*lexis*)"[2].

It must not be overlooked that there exists a second or paired substantive component of ancient Greek politics alongside action, namely speech, that it is action accompanied by and related to speech, speech and action together that create the conception of ancient Greek politics, as opposed to action alone. Indeed, in following Arendt's conceptualization of ancient Greek politics, speech as part of the political should not be thought of as some secondary component within it, but rather that speech is paired with action appearing at the same time to produce politics, existing as a substantial condition of it taking place. This is the second component of politics beyond action, or rather when appearing at the same time as action.

Speech and action thus form lines within a multiplicity creating an assemblage, which assemblage is politics if one takes a Deleuzian understanding of such coupling. The relation by which such lines of multiplicity within the art of ancient Greek politics assemble themselves into assemblages and by which they relate to and create one another is articulated by Arendt in her definition of action, that, "finding the right words at the right moment, quite apart from the information or communication they may convey, is action."[3] Thus action in its substantive nature and component of politics is the ability to speak, the ability to convey and communicate something at the right moment. It is at this point that the connection between action and speech become coupled with and tied up in an appearance of politics that is conceptualized by Arendt to be non-other than the ancient condition of Greek politics; the two together, one serving and yielding to the other.

It is at this point that we begin to glimpse a preliminary

diagram of how an understanding of the ancient Greek conceptualization of politics might be tied to an understanding of
Occidental architecture, namely that it resides, like politics in
ancient Greece, in and on action on the one hand and communication on the other. To take this conceptual glimpse to an extrapolative continuation, it could be asserted that the substantive
content of Occidental architecture is nothing other than the same
two primary qualities of ancient Greek politics – action and
communication – thus defining architecture's existential essence
as a formative condition of politics, or at least existing on the
same plane as politics. It is through understanding the
substantive condition and nature of politics in ancient Greece
that we can begin to draw an analogy of it with architecture and
with the assertion regarding architecture's existence within a
political life-world with which we commenced. This is at least a
possibility if we collapse the ancient Greek conceptualization of
politics as discussed by Arendt and relate it to architecture's
arguable substantive condition.

In continuing with the conception of ancient Greek politics,
when action coupled with speech appears it requires by necessity
a space to do so; the consequence of action and speech appearing
in space produces and defines a certain quality and type of space
that Arendt terms the "public realm". This is so, "because of
[action's] inherent tendency to disclose the agent together with
the act, it needs for its full appearance the shining brightness we
once called glory, and which is possible only in the public
realm."[4] The coupling of action and speech is only affected in a
third medium, which is spatial.

Within the very essence of the conception of ancient Greek
politics is a spatiality through which politics might be performed
in and identified as such. Without the spatial aspect of action and
speech, politics remains mute and ceases to eventuate. By
necessity therefore, and as a consequence of this understanding,
action and speech are further coupled with a third line, which is

the presence of a performance, which is to say space, creating in turn and as a result the public realm. For politics to appear and occur it requires space as a third assembling component, and the resultant assemblage of these three multiplicities, action, speech and space, is none other than what the ancient Greeks termed the "public realm".

The nature of the public realm is one in which action and speech occur, or in our analogical continuity with concerns architectural, where praxis (action) and communication occur. In a continuation of our extrapolation of ancient Greek politics with architecture, and in a parlance that might be more familiar to architects, we might translate the ancient Greek concept of the public realm by which politics is created and affected as the architectural "site". Such a conception of the architectural site as being one where politics is played out might not be too unfamiliar to architects.

If we take Arendt's analysis of ancient Greek politics as outlined above, the public realm or public space is indeed an identifiable site of politics to us moderns as well, but only becomes a political site in which politics is played out as a result of praxis and speaking (or communication) appearing, be it architectural or not. Public space, or the "public realm" is thus "the space within the world which men need in order to appear at all, [and] is therefore more specifically "the work of man"", than is "the work of his hands or the labor of his body"[5].

Public space cannot be characterized by particular size, material, fabrication or creation of something as typology, such as a square, street, boulevard, avenue or building resultant as they are of physical labor and the "work of man's hands", but rather the architectural *conception* or intellectual creation that creates a *content* for space regardless of how small or large that space might be is what the essence of public space is: it is a realm where action and communication (speech) play themselves out. Public space regardless of its area and typology, and it could indeed be exceedingly small as a room, is defined by communicative praxis in appearance, or by extrapolative analogy, "architecture" in other terms. It is this which Arendt terms the "work of man": a particular type and quality of space.

The creation and coming about of the public realm or public space is a consequence of people living together. Only when we exist in a society with other people do we have a space that can be deemed public, where action and communication (speech) appear and are witnessed. The public realm requires spectators to see an act and hear speech in order for it to be public – only as a result of seeing, hearing and witnessing something in a place does a space become public. Indeed, in order for politics to exist we need others, we need a shared time and space for action to be seen; for speech and communication to be heard we need listeners and responders, that is other people present and interacting in some manner with the speaker in the same place – even if only listening or viewing.

Arendt in fact inverts the notion of the necessity of action and communication to be seen and heard for public space to come about. She writes that to live among men, we need action[6], that is that action as a substantive component of politics is a necessity of people living together, that politics as a phenomena is a natural occurrence governed by nothing other than people living together, and that wherever they may live together politics appears, and that the fundamental condition of people living together is the necessity of politics appearing. It is this condition of action as a substantive component of society that Arendt terms *vita activa*, or the activity of man. One of the activities of man in the fellowship of other men, indeed the necessity of such fellowship is politics.

Everything we thus do in society in front of and in the vicinity of other people might be considered as political action. When we speak, build, communicate and appear amongst others, a certain space is created that becomes public, which is pregnant with politics.

Conceiving of and executing architecture is none other. As soon as the architect conceives of doing something on a site, regardless of whether it might be insignificant or momentous, triumphal or banal, a process is activated that leads substantially to politics coming about. It is impossible to build architecture without entering onto the terrain of the political, and it is for this reason, following Arendt's conceptualization of ancient Greek politics, that architecture might be deemed first and foremost a political act.

The action that the architect takes in his/her hands when designing a building or a space releases processes and formations for living, it releases action and communication, both spoken and received – two substances that lie at the heart of the ancient Greek conceptualization of politics – which in turn create public space. It is a question of releasing something, of releasing processes through action and communication. Arendt indeed refers to "action" in *The Human Condition* as "the releasing of processes"[7], and when action and communication are released, space will not remain the same; it is this emergence of difference or the releasing of processes in space that is the mark of politics which architecture can't escape.

In turning from the ancient Greeks and their conceptualization of politics to the post-Roman society of that of medieval times, we read in Thomas Aquinas' writing that, "Man is by nature political, that is social"[8]. By medieval times the concept of politics shifts from the necessity of action and speech occurring in space to simply being a fundamentally accepted condition of man as a result of her living in society. This conception of the political differs to an extent from that of the ancient Greek conceptualization of it, where something had to appear and as a result be communicated.

Aquinas' conceptualization of politics equates and draws into each other the meaning of the terms "political" and "social". The conception of such politics is that because Man lives amongst other Men, by default s/he exists in the realm of politics and partakes in it. In this conception nothing else is required for the political to come about than the presence of others, of other people. It is the interaction between people within society that by necessity creates the space and appearance of the political concept in the medieval age.

Thus the conceptualization of politics shifts in medieval times from the action-speech-space assemblage of the ancient Greeks to the interactive condition and potential of simply being with and amongst others. Such a conception of politics translates to the understanding that nothing else is needed for its appearance than the community of people. In this medieval understanding then, everything that architects might do within society and for society is connected with other people and for the benefit of other people, and as such by default enters the realm of a social product and hence also the realm of politics.

As architects conceiving architecture, if it is not for the benefit of other people and their use and enjoyment, there is no purpose in creating it. Architecture by definition is concealed and grounded in social servitude: it is because other people exist, and that we exist together with other people, and that there is a communal necessity to what we do, that we build. Without society, architecture would have never emerged, as there would be no need to house, shelter, serve the needs of or communicate anything at all to others.

Architecture by default results from a social condition, from the fact of people living together and hence in this understanding occupies the space of the political – not only in theory, but also in practice. Thus if architecture is both created by and bounded by the fact of society, then according to Aquinas' conceptualization of politics, architecture is of nothing other in substance than an element of the political, and a profoundly political activity at that.

Moving on from Aquinas and his conceptualization of politics to the age of reason and the rise of the scientific worldview, the emerging age of proto-technology and proto-capitalism, the conceptualization of politics shifts again. With the emergence of science and technology politics becomes conceptualized as what Arendt terms, "the art of man"[9]. Here, politics becomes seen as something machinic that man has put in place and which begins to perform and live an auto-machinic nature, producing government and the execution of government for the common good as a machine. Commonwealths, states, and within them judiciaries and other mechanisms of government are conceived of as an artful machine performing according to type for the serving of justice, representation of polity and the execution of law.

Such change in the conceptualization of politics in the age of proto-capitalism results from humans becoming what Arendt terms *homo faber*, that is concealed in a metaphysics of primarily being a maker of things. As humanity's metaphysics alters from the medieval period to the proto-capitalist era, so does our conceptualization of politics. Politics becomes a form of art, more precisely an art of man, which directly corresponds to all our other activities as a maker of tools and machines, forming a direct connection with the emergence of a scientific worldview. It is this scientific worldview which transforms occidental humanity from the *homo activa* of the Greek world to the *homo faber* of our present time.

Arendt creates this conceptual shift of politics by placing the emergence of political philosophy in the seventeenth and eighteenth centuries to the emergence of a scientific world view, that is bound-up with a practice of what Man can do with nature (observe, measure and ultimately control it). As Man begins to control his/her nature and subtract making from it, s/he can do the same with politics as a fabrication in the service of people. In this sense politics becomes an artifice, which Arendt likens to the paradigm of the watch and the watchmaker[10]: politics becomes a machine.

The analogy between politics as a machine and the conception of architecture as a machine, and hence an activity resembling the machinations of the political, comes to fruition perceptively in the nineteenth and twentieth centuries. Before the rise of the Modern Movement as an obviously machinic oeuvre, even before mechanization had fully developed during the second half of the nineteenth century, we see architecture being utilized as a machine of representation for and by the state as a medium between it and its institutions and the populace it governed by way of the re-emergence of classicist order in Neoclassicism and what it conveyed to society at large as representation: buildings as representational machines. Although it took a number of centuries for the proto-technological world to transform building into capitalist scales of economics, by the early-twentieth century architecture was indeed not only figuratively, but literally seen as a machine, both in its production if we consider Gropius' conceptualization of it, and in both in function if we consider Le Corbusier's phrase conceptualizing modern architecture as a "machine for living", not to mention his Unité de Habitation or his work in Chandrigah.

The machinic order of metaphysics as reflected in the development of politics is echoed in architecture between the seventeenth century leading up into and particularly the nineteenth and twentieth centuries. Architecture in these centuries became a mirror held-up to the workings of the modern economic state and condition of its society, and extended that society's political-social-economic condition in their built output. By the nineteenth and early-twentieth century the machinic conceptualization of politics and the condition of society that had thus been created in centuries preceding, explicitly catches up with and infuses architectural conception, sensibility and production with the advent of the Modern Movement and the International Style.

In drawing the preliminary discussion of the conceptualization of politics and its analogical relation to architecture to a
pause, whether one conceives of politics in the vein of action and
speech requiring space, or whether one conceives of it as the
condition of man as a result of society, or indeed building
likened to a machine for governing and ordering society, the sum
effect of all the above conceptions is that politics sets off affects,
sensate responses by which it necessarily operates, and does so
in space. In this sense it is not so alien to the condition of –
indeed a parallel might be drawn with – architecture, which
finds itself as the potential creator of affects in space. Thus potentially both politics and architecture perform for the creation of
presences, and it is this "affective" potentiality of architecture
vis-à-vis its base condition – even medium of politics – that
might be deemed as the promise of its substantive condition,
which is a political one at its heart.

Politics, Architecture and Activism

If we follow Peter Eisenman's argument pertaining to architecture and affect in his essay "The Affects of Singularity" we read that "affect in architecture is the sensate response to a physical environment"[1], it is the feeling of a presence, that which may be termed the heart of action and speech. The affective potential and possibility of architecture given its substantive analogical nature with politics is its ability to activate presence and sensate responses, to begin to perform sonorously beyond its material nature, this is what Eisenman identifies as strong media[2].

In his essay "The Affects of Singularity", Eisenman identifies two types of media, weak media and strong media, of which architecture formerly occupied the later, but has since fallen into the category of the former. Eisenman writes that:

> Throughout the nineteenth century, there is a development of architecture for mass society parallel to the development of the new political state, [and that this] modern political state of the late eighteenth century and early-nineteenth century corresponded to the rise of social and economic institutions and with the beginning of the change of architecture from strong media to weak media.[3]

As modern political development began to take hold and the modern state required media to communicate its message, architecture began to lose ground, and indeed has since entirely lost ground on the territory that it had formerly occupied as strong media. Modern political development and its form of communication or form of speaking bypassed architecture as a medium from around this time onwards, and instead embraced predominantly two-dimensional media such as journalism and print, furthering it in the twentieth century with radio, television and the internet, leaving architecture to occupy a space outside that of political media it had previously enjoyed.

In this sense, since the rise of modern politics and the nation state, and despite the analogy of the machine between modern politics and modern architecture, architecture has increasingly lost its political rationale as a medium, it has become ineffective as a medium, it has become weak in its possibility for communicating political messages and creating affect. Eisenman writes further that, "while strong media as architecture was about affect, strong media today in terms of commercial television and journalism is basically concerned with effect: how quickly, compactly and distinctly can the message get across?"[4]

Although the historic potential and possibility of architecture lies within the realm of strong media tied to the political message and acting as politics, in our present time this is not the case. In order for architecture to become political again, an organ of politics, it needs to reassert its condition as a strong media, it needs to begin to produce affect again; and to begin to produce presence and sensate responses as a result of its actualization it needs a political sensibility. Architecture once more needs to become truly political in order to become affective, and it is this which is the potential and possibility, even promise of architecture.

Instead of lying down and accepting the fate of contemporary late-twentieth century architecture as an altogether weak, ineffective, hollow form of communication as Eisenman argues, architecture instead should be raised to the potential of politics yet again, to a medium that produces political presences, feelings, new thoughts, to a medium that creates sensate responses, becomes deployed to the purposes of apprehending and suspending a user's subjectivity, and in turn revealing something new in a user's experience and relation to society, space and the city – to a medium that communicates, and which communicative message in my argument and in the argument of "strong media" is of a political nature. Architecture in this politically charged sense of production might then come to be thought of as a guerrilla practice in the context of the urban landscape, and for this we need more than just the dictates of capitalism within architecture production, we need to turn architecture production into forms of activism, and this precisely because the political message in our time is conveyed entirely by print, electronic, digital and broadcast media.

Although throughout the nineteenth, twentieth and beginning of the twenty-first century, architecture, or more precisely the production of certain architects or movements within architecture, has sought-out the political for its process of conception, and sought the reflection or mediation of politics by way of its function and form. However admirable and worthwhile these practices have been, they have remained burdened by the condition of architecture as an increasingly weak media in relation to other media on offer for politics, and because of this the mere exercising of function and form – despite their often political genesis and intention of outcome – has also remained weak.

Amongst such architects and movements in our recent past that have attempted to convey the political through their practice and who have created distinctly politically charged forms of architecture we might cite certain examples of the work of the Modern Movement in the 1920s and '30s, the International Style championed by Phillip Johnson and Henry Russell Hitchcock on which most of our early post-war office space was modeled, the work of Team X and Alison and Peter Smithson with their concrete Brutalist aesthetics the likes of the Barbican just outside the City of London and the Queen Elizabeth Hall and Hayward Gallery of Southbank in London to name but three examples, and of course other lesser known practices and sites.

Such examples have sought to capture the political and charge their making with a condition approaching the releasing of affect-infusing strength into their communication. However, in relation to the strength and meaning of *activism* as politics *par excellence* they fell short, precisely because architectural form has since lost the strength of conveying the political message in comparison to the strength of television or print-media: the strength of their articulation was lesser in comparison to other politically charged media, and it is in the strength of articulation that we can define activism occurring as such.

The mid-late twentieth and even early-twenty first century hasn't been shy of producing other forms of politically charged architecture, but of an altogether less admirable genesis of conception. Amongst these we could cite the Israeli settlement building that Rafi Segal and Eyal Weizman have analyzed. Another example of highly politically charged architecture in this period might be the parade space of the Nuremberg rallies of Nazi Germany and its architecture of light. Other architecture of the political variety of our recent past that might be cited is architecture swamped and dictated by planning regulations as a result of political rules. However, none of these examples are activist in the sense of its definition of changing and challenging the status quo for the purpose of producing other sensative affective responses on which social order might change.

In all of the above instances of politically charged architecture of our recent past, the work produced came to reinforce the status quo and the politics of the state as opposed to challenge it or apprehend it. It is clear to see why these examples of archi-tecture, despite occupying a level of strength within their media, fail to be classified as activist, namely because they are in conformity with the politics of the state as opposed to mediating a political message that might release affect in opposition to the status quo and thus create worthwhile change.

So if truly political architecture of the "strong" media variety might be defined as activist architecture, that which challenges the status quo of society in a worthwhile manner, requiring a stronger method or medium of communication than which the Modern Movement, Team X and other contemporary individual practices have achieved to date, and if it is of an opposite relation to the architecture of the political status quo, then how might activism in architecture be defined? To answer such question the very nature and strategy of activism as a strong media needs to be discussed and examples given.

The reason for the rise of activism as *énoncé* of political action in our time is the consequence of contemporary politics itself. Contemporary politics has given way from producing sensate, affective outcomes toward accommodating government through measures of pragmatism. The politics of our contemporary status quo is a pragmatist politics represented by the philosophical branch of *Pragmatism* ascendant from the late-nineteenth century, characterized by a politics that is neither too radical nor too conservative, as long as it works and delivers for the largest number of constituents. This constituency in turn has come to increasingly occupy the middle ground and in turn switch off into apathy, a middle and lower-middle class which on the whole in industrially and socially developed countries expects very little from politics and public discourse. It is a centrist management of society and of the economy and public affairs which commands such *realpolitik*.

In light of such a luke-warm and bland state of affairs in public life and discourse, and indeed in the state of affairs of architecture on the whole and of the public realm, an injection of strength is required that shakes this apathetic Goldilocks zone of subjectivity toward something more perceptive. This shaking can only be done justice to through activism, action which is strong, sensate and produces affect.

In order for architecture to become strong and communicative and thus political again, it requires architecture to shift itself out of its bland topiary of pragmatism in which most of the indistinguishable contemporary commercial architecture of today is produced, toward architecture that produces sensate responses again.

One example and strategy for returning architecture to activism and thus to politics and strong media is to go against the grain of functional, corporate typology and capitalist sensibilities and its politics within architecture, and to begin to introduce strategies such as the Situationists' concept of *detournement*, whereby unexpected, sensately out of place yet familiar elements were proposed to be used to create potential for situations.

Detournement roughly translates from the French verb *detourner*, which means to divert, making the meaning of *detournement* translatable as that which is "diversionary"[5]. *Detournement* is a practice bound up in distorting and diverting meaning from expected forms of representation and figuration, thus acting as a critique and displacement of representation in a way that the results become harnessed for a site of resistance to political representation, one that deconstructs representation, and in the process critiques the representation of politics, including the politics of architecture. Others have termed it as "satirical parody"[6] or a form of disorientation and confrontation, whereby the condition that a work is supposed to convey is turned upside-down through parody and satire to create an affect of disorientation and confrontation – a sort of anti-architecture.

In the practice of *detournement*, a critique is enabled that critiques the politics and use of a space in its very nature of being; an effective critique thus produces a strong affect thus occupying the space of strong media, and by consequence is of an activist nature. In architecture, the harnessing and consequential mixing of an entire palate of existing architectural and/or graphic vocabulary opens spaces up to be read differently, and to affect different sensations to its users, but must be done so in a way that creates blatantly strong affects in order to achieve activism. Such examples abound in graphic design and pop-art, to name the work of Banksy as one, or anonymous stencil artists in our cities and some cartoonists as others.

Other existing strategies might borrow, for example, from the late-Stephen Perella's HyperSurface theory in architecture, whereby the surface of architecture was proposed to work together with the media image – the present-day strong media – and incorporate it into the fabric of an architecture, indeed create the architecture by way of it, whilst at the same time deconstructing both it and the architecture that it enabled. This second example contains the proposition of capturing existing strong media and inverting it for the purposes of an architectural language – such examples of architecture production are emergent in some particular instances of the work of Coop-Himmelblau, Lars Spuybroek, Diller + Scofidio, Kas Oosterhuis and Ilona Lénard and others.

Beyond these above examples mentioned, numerous other strategies can be invented to bring political affect back to architecture production. However, regardless of what strategy might be employed, architecture as an activist project of production requires an altogether different sensibility of approach to it than that which exists in the profession at large today.

Eisenman writes of the possibility of returning architecture to strong media by saying that, "a possible way of returning architecture to the realm of affect may not be through the idea of the individual or expressive, or through any kind of standardization or repetition of the norm, but in fact through an idea of singularity."[7] Such "singularity", according to Eisenman, is the putting to forefront the "thisness" of a thing[8], of creating spaces that are not necessarily forms of expressionism, but contain the thisness of a thing, condition or percept in a blatant form, and as a result activate built material in space with content, making it affective and active. The question, however, is what the content of such affective architecture might be; to this one must answer that it needs to communicate, speak, act and produce perceptive difference – not merely material thisness – in order to be activist.

Bernard Tschumi has said of architecture that it occupies the social space of "timeless servitude to the King"[9], with this King having alternately been religion, metaphysics, the state – and now capitalism in our current time. What such servitude suggests is precisely the attitude of that which we commenced with, namely the perception and contemporary practice of providing functional shelter for work, living and other daily uses of humans within the context of the capitalist economics of outlay and return, pragmatism adhering to the dictates of the profit motive. The call of returning politics to architecture and beginning an activist stance through architecture production is precisely a call to break such servitude to the present King, namely capitalism, and to perhaps conceive of things that might not be strictly functional or responsive to budget constraints, but go against the grain and begin to create affect. Such a call is for a different type and condition of architecture and space, to place architecture once again in an active situation of communication, to activate the production of architecture.

Why such call for activism in architecture, why the need for activism in architecture?

Returning to Arendt, the reason there is need and calling for activism in architecture is that, "the things that owe themselves exclusively to men [in this essay thinking about architecture and spatial intervention] …constantly condition their human makers."[10] Architecture, as a thing that owes itself exclusively to men, regardless of the type of architecture conceived, "constantly condition their human makers". Modern corporate and consumerist architecture conditions its human makers albeit in a different way to architecture that begins to become politically affective and communicative. The question is, what sort of conditioning do architects want to leave behind and put in place as a result of their efforts, is it a conditioning that serves the dictates of capitalism or consumerism and is subservient to it, or is it of an entirely different conditioning type, one that attempts to change the subjectivity of users, to cause them to think new thoughts and feel new feelings? The conditioning that activist architecture calls for is a radical release of different ways of thinking and feeling about something, different ways of seeing, using and ultimately acting in turn. It is this which activism in architecture and spatial disciplines calls itself to and results in. This should be the *raison d'etre* of architecture, to return architecture to the realm of the political.

Activism in architecture, the making of things for the affective realization of politics creates an alteration in subjectivity precisely because humans are conditioned by things, or in Arendt's words because "human existence is conditioned existence, it would be impossible without things, and things would be a heap of unrelated articles, a non-world, if they were not the conditioners of human existence."[11] The call of activism in architecture is for the architect to begin to think politically about their making and consciously place in the forefront of their architecture a political message or political affect, to activate their architecture with communication in a way that the user begins to feel and think differently about something, that the user's subjectivity is suspended and apprehended for a moment, and an affective presence makes itself felt.

In qualifying such activist stance in architecture production, and in borrowing from Arendt in regards to qualifying the term "action", Arendt writes that "...action is the political activity par excellence..."[12] with "action" being defined as "beginning something new"[13]. Thus activism as a politically charged architectural stance is precisely about beginning something new, of releasing yet unseen possibilities and processes into the world: an activation of something that by necessity is a political activity as such. Arendt continues, that "....as a result of action being the political activity par excellence, ...natality [birth], not mortality, may be the central category of the political..."[14] Natality or birth, the starting of something over, the beginning again of something, the bringing to surface of things latent and placing them into an active presence to create affect is the heart of the political, and it is this that should be the calling of architecture and its potential and possibility.

Given the call for activism in architecture in order to make architecture affective, how does activism in architecture work, how can it be conceived? Of all the various art forms, Arendt writes that, "...theatre is the political art par excellence; only there is the political sphere of human life transposed into art."[15] Such a statement might suggest that architecture cannot achieve the political as it is outside the realm of theater as a form, this might be surmised due to the fact that theater as an art form combines action and speaking, action and communication, whilst architecture does not. Conversely to this sentiment, one might begin to conceive architecture as a *form* of theater for the purposes of pursuing a political activity through it – that is to place communication into the forefront of the architectural conception in a way that communication begins to play itself out as a result of the architectural.

The task therefore that one might suggest for activist architecture is to create a percept of theater through architecture, that is space or spaces where action and communication combine and result in something playing itself out. It might even be conceptualized that activism in architecture is created when architecture becomes substantive theater; when we produce architecture in the vein of theater.

To examine the substantive nature of theater and to relate it to architecture, to understand and conceptualize what it is that is being called for in creating activist architecture, theater might be said to consist of an interaction or double-combined play of communication and action, of communicating and acting at the same time *creating* the medium. Active architecture, activated architecture, architecture that activates, or in another term activist architecture requires a similar double-combined play of communication coupled with action to become affective. In order to achieve this architecture needs to become sonorous, and for this it needs a language, a particular palate of communication that begins to speak, and thus create affect. To forward an understanding of how this might be achieved, one needs to understand the substantive nature of action and speech.

Arendt writes of action and speech that, "action and speech need the surrounding presence of others"[16], this is to say that it only occurs where other people are present, that is first it requires other people, and secondly it requires a shared space for that presence. In essence, this is what the "public realm" is, the creation of the public realm by way of others hearing, seeing and witnessing action and speech. Architecture as theater and as politics, that is activist architecture needs the shared space of the "surrounding presence of others" as a mechanism for political affect. Because it needs the "surrounding presence of others" its most apt place of appearance would be in the city – this is the first condition of activist architecture. As a result of it being in the city in the surrounding presence of others, it begins to satisfy some of the requirements of theater, namely the presence of others, and begins to create an act along the lines of the affect of theater.

The nature of architecture in the context of the city is a form of fabrication that "is surrounded by and in constant contact with the world"[17], and thus takes on the contexts of the city as a setting for its play, for the playing-out of affect. The urban context becomes the scenography as it were of the architectural language employed.

The conceptualization of action and speech, not dissimilarly, might be characterized as "surrounded by and in constant contact with the web of the acts and words of other men."[18] Thus activist fabrications in an urban context as a political activity, similarly to action and speech, require a form of interaction to be enabled, a putting in place of constant contact and feedback with and by the people who witness it. It is this interaction between a fabrication and the users that activates the language of it to be heard and perceived. The language of a particular architecture becomes affective as a result of the interaction occurring.

In order for architecture to become an activist fabrication, an affective fabrication, in order for it to activate itself, it needs to leave something in its nature behind, it needs to morph from being mere fabrication toward being something that is inter-active in nature, something that causes its language to become affect. It is as a result of the causation of affect that fabrication or architecture enters the political realm. Activist architecture therefore is in opposition to everything one conceives tradi-tionally as representative of the discipline of architecture, it performs differently, its functions and forms are different, and its entire paradigm is other to the point where it might not even have plumbing – or maybe only have plumbing. To achieve such percept, to tie architecture and fabrication to the substantive nature of speech and action, is the challenge of activist architecture. Tying architecture production or fabrication to the ability to communicate is the second condition of activist architecture.

How is architecture's condition of communication created or, in other words, how might we further an activist architecture? In answering this we can turn to Andrew Benjamin's portrayal of architecture in his first chapter of *Architectural Philosophy*, where he surmises that function (and with it architecture), is always tied to a condition of repetition, be it of program or of time, and that it is this repetition which makes function possible[19]. The question, however, in the communicative ability of architecture, and hence of the possibility of activist architecture, is precisely how might this repetition of function and time be suspended, altered or disturbed; how might otherness or alterity be introduced into function? In order for otherness and alterity to be introduced into the repetition of function, the program and with it function must be negated, so that a different space of time and form emerge. Once alterity or otherness is introduced into repetition, an opening occurs in function that destabilizes form. It is this destabilization that becomes the mark of alterity or otherness, and the possibility for communication to arise within the users of the space. The introduction of alterity in relation to function and program is thus the third condition of activist architecture.

Given program, repetition and function as precursors to architecture, and the question how might these elements of architecture be altered, we naturally arrive at a position whereby we might alter program, repetition and function to the extent that we might be operating outside the realms of architecture altogether, or perhaps in the realm of an anti-architecture of sorts if vestiges of them are sustained as far as function is concerned.

If indeed these elements that make architecture are reduced to near zero, whereby even function becomes compromised or suspended, what we are left with to sculpt is the excess of architecture, which is signification. In such circumstances signification of what is built becomes the function, and with it we are reaching closer to pure communication as a hallmark of activism.

The presence and promotion of signification beyond and above function in a way that function is prescribed and tied to signification opens up the possibility for real communication to occur. Activist architecture therefore enters the realm of architecture where function is subservient to signification, and hence communication takes over as reason for program.

At this point some might argue that architecture, and with it function, is being exited, and an anti-architecture is being pursued. Such a premise is correct if we aim to create communication through architecture in order for it to become affective, for it is in the strength of signification, and a signification of critique and disjunction, that architecture begins to become activist.

As Lyotard writes in *Libidinal Economy*, "there is no sign or thought of the sign which is not about power and for power."[20] It is precisely this character of signification that leads such architecture to become strong media: one needs power, or more precisely force, for activism to work. Power without activist disjunction, however, remains within the realm of the State. For this reason it is the creation of the disjuncted sign, and through it a critique of power that is required, that is to say a force of communication critiquing power, which is the fourth condition for activist architecture.

Arendt writes that, "a production process necessarily precedes the actual existence of every object"[21], this is to say that for every way of receiving, there is a way of putting together[22]. The key to activist architecture and fabrication is the way something is put together for the purposes of a particular reception. After all, this is what communication is. Activist architecture as a result of its necessity for interaction as a requirement for its language to become activated and create affect requires a particular way of putting together, it requires conditions approaching an anti-architecture in the traditional sense.

The way something is put together, the conceptual production process preceding the actual existence of the fabrication is at the very heart of activist architecture, of making architecture affective. To borrow words from Marcos Novak:

> ...all making is political, not in a crude, literal sense, but in the very fiber of its being. What something represents is usually indifferent....What something is, what constellations of practices have brought it into being, what rhizomatic structural relationships it has to its multiple contexts, how strong a "meaning magnet" it is, or how reflective an "interpretation screen" it is, are all political aspects. All making is a microcosmic exercise in envisioning alternative worlds. Our

constructs and interactions embody values and imply social orders, whether we are aware of this or not.[23]

It is precisely these sentiments and their putting to use that courses through the vein of how activist architecture might be realized.

Examples that could be cited of fabrication approaching activism might be the work of English artist Banksy, who uses the urban fabric, the surfaces of walls, buildings and infrastructure to couple with his urban art of political nature. It is not the art work in itself that activates the political in his work, however provocative it may be, but the coupling of the entire visual ensemble within a given urban fabric which creates the communication, the affect of presence, or sensate response in the viewers mind – it is the language of expression *coupled* with the context of where and how that language is performed. In this way, Banksy's work hijacks the urban topos to inject it with media of a political nature – this is one instance of activist fabrication.

Other attempts at political architecture have also been attempted by instance in the London + 10 project[24] of the AA School of Architecture, whereby the fabrication of something, an act, a condition, a presence or sensate response was created in public space and filmed for posterity. Although this second example didn't explicitly always utilize built fabrication, its results did achieve political and/or social communication, the communication of presences and sensate responses.

Both of these examples engage the urban environment in a theater of process, and activate architecture as a revealing of process creating activism, depositing an affect of that process as an end result, which might be deemed as political. It is this engagement with activating processes that is the mark of activist architecture. As Arendt writes, "Processes, therefore, and not ideas and models and shapes of things to be, become the guide for the making and fabricating of activities of *homo faber* in the modern age."[25]

Architecture once embodied the highest artistic creation of man, the mother of all arts as it were. Since the rise of the scientific age architecture has steadily decreased in relevance to the point today where architecture is merely seen as a way of ordering function, providing shelter, or facilitating capitalist return. Much of what goes on in many architecture schools today echoes this state of affairs. Architecture was once the communicating vessel of world view, of culture, a central pivot in civilization that people read and learnt from about culture and world view. Perhaps, as Victor Hugo wrote, "this will kill that"[26], the rise of new media and specifically that of printing will kill off architecture in as far as the communication of knowledge and culture is concerned. This foresight has largely fulfilled itself, with periodic movements of architecture where it temporarily regained some strength to heave a cultural communication once more, such as in the Modern Movement.

What architecture as activism has the potential of achieving is the remaking of relevance of architecture, of placing it once more for a while in a position where it acts as a communicating vessel, a vessel with relevance for human subjectivity, thought, behavior and action that it once occupied. It is only through politically activating architecture as a vessel for activism, and a political one at that, that it has the hope of evacuating irrelevance as a cultural form and recoup a losing of ground.

The Promise of the Politics of Digital Architecture

To frame "digital architecture" and its theories by the question of politics is a question that may follow a reading of Hannah Arendt's argument contained in *The Human Condition*, one of asking what action and effect on action digital architecture produces, generates and leaves behind. Such a question is one of asking digital architecture, "What actions, thoughts and feelings does it produce; what does it speak?"

It is questionable whether many architects involved in the digital, parametric turn of architecture have asked themselves this question. On the whole, digital architecture practices have been a way toward finding and articulating form and surface in ever-increasing novel ways, of breaking the canon of the International Style and that of the Post-Modernist style, of integrating new forms of visualization resultant from technological advances as opposed to beginning to ask the question of what sort of effects and affects such architecture might hope to produce. However, in framing the question of digital or computational architecture as a question of politics, it is precisely the question of *action* resultant from and within a particular computationally derived practice of architecture that is at stake.

An entry into interrogating the substance of digital architecture's politics, or rather the promise of such architecture's politics, can be approached from an understanding of the sentiments contained in the sentence, "For every way of receiving there is a way of putting together". The understanding contained in such approach to architecture is an understanding of intended explicit communication in and through one's architecture derived directly from the result of the methods of its assembly. Such a question is one of asking computational architecture: what does it speak? Ways of putting together for the purpose of an intended communication might have in their sight ways of structuring work, leisure, the everyday, or alternatively merely forwarding a reading of architecture's internal, self-referential discourse-practice, but nonetheless all in some way producing a "receiving" or way to action within and from the built fabric as a result of a particular putting together and consequential valorizing of communication.

That the possibility of creating a particular way of receiving exists within the practice of architecture is not in doubt, for it is this amongst the many facets that make up architecture, and that make it a civilizational performing vessel of communication in the first place. Action resultant from the creation of communication or an intended way of receiving leading to particular types of action, by necessity derive from and rest upon the way one begins to structure a putting together resulting in a specific receival, that is the creation of, and a structuring of, a politics of architecture. It is the interplay between an intended explicit communication on the one hand, and derivative action on the other, which results in a generating and playing out of a politics resultant from a particular way of putting together, which is architecture's potential. This is evident in architecture ranging from the medieval stonemasons' practice of Gothic architecture and the derivative subjectivization and consequential action it derived in its users, Neo-Classical facades of public institutions of the Enlightened nineteenth century state and their derivative communication and subjectivization of the relation between citizen and state, through to Le Corbusier's way of putting together a "machine for living" and its impact on the subjectivization of everyday modern life.

That digital architecture and its architects have yet to identify an intended content of communication and intended reformulation of action resultant from and derivative of their specific way of putting together beyond pursuing the indeed very important civilizational questions contained in advanced technological fabrication and making, might evidence that their politics of making finds its ends and exhausts itself in a scientific rationale without any criticality of our culture's many patho-logical contextual and social productions, and rather merely serves as an extension of the contemporary capitalist order and cultural logic of bourgeois regimes, as opposed to being involved in any critical reflection and potential of their work. Such a position is not extraordinary given its echo of Bernard Tschumi's sentiments that architecture is a practice of "timeless servitude to the King"[1].

But the fact that architecture, including digital architecture, has a promise and potential for politics is undeniable, and in the context of digital architecture's servitude to the spectacle, by way of its servitude to the contemporary capitalist order, is ever more imperative. In fact all architecture, whether of the spectacle or not, is involved by default in a production of effects and feeling, and thus is political in its very nature. The question therefore becomes: just what sort of politics might computational or digital architecture lend itself to, or rather have the potential for valorizing beyond the mere servitude of the spectacle by which it is captured?

To answer this question the term *"poiesis"* needs to be requisi-tioned and an understanding of a particular way of putting together articulated, which results in the production of different effects. The term *poiesis* derives from Aristotle's *Poetics*, which details instructions as to the type and nature of linguistic production that might create poetry in the course of bringing about certain genres of drama, namely tragedy, comedy and the epic, and with it particular types of effects and action. Each of these genres is derived from different types of linguistic production creating different types of effect, and in producing different kinds of effect the linguistic production is derivative of different forms of *poiesis*.

We see that the concept of *poiesis* is directly tied to production and to action, and furthermore that it is tied to the production of different types of effect, that is to say that it operates as a political vehicle by way of communication. Digital architecture as a way of putting together, as a way of *poiesis,* contains the potential for a particular type of affect producing. The question of digital architecture's potential for communication and consequential way of putting together is one of what is latent within the *poiesis* of its generative machine, the computer; it is the resolution of a question that asks, "Just what sort of effect is inherent within the promise of digitally induced built fabric?" or, "Just what kind of *poiesis* might the promise of digital architecture by virtue and recourse to its machinic source bring about, or have potential for bringing about?"

The promise of the politics of computational architecture involves and is derived from the nature and type of communication (affects) achieved by the inherent act of utilizing the computational machine. This production is potentially limitless in scope, the effects being produced can take on any number of forms and related affects (depending on the variation, difference and combination of scripts) tending toward an infinite combination – this is the latent inherency of the computational machine's *poiesis.* The computational politics of digital architecture thus ultimately, and in its most immediate outcome of *poiesis,* lends itself to and contains the promise of an infinite variety of affective constructs precisely due to the computer's inherent "way of putting together". The inherency of such infinitesimal ways of putting together produces a politics of digital architecture that cannot but be described otherwise than the potential for the production of endless heterogeneity above and beyond all other considerations of effect; it is to this heterogeneity that computational use lends itself most immediately in digital architecture production, which contains the seeds of a potential politics of the typology to play out.

The question and creative aim of the politics of computational architecture or computational poetics in architecture should therefore be that which is inherent within its *poiesis'* promise, namely the endless production of heterogeneity, difference and endless worlds of possibility. Within this endless heterogeneity and possibility for difference, there will unavoidably and necessarily exist what Deleuze and Guattari characterized as spaces of smooth character (nomad effects) and spaces of striated character (effects derivative of work, money and history), with the two constantly interacting with each other creating the beauty of life. It is for this that computational politics in architecture has the inherent promise, and this due to the structure of its *poiesis*, both on the social level of the built environment pertaining to work and history and on its practice relating to built surface and form, which create the place of function for its social use.

The endless production of heterogeneity consists of the production of singularities as its yield. Singularities are lines that Deleuze and Guattari have termed as that which constitute the subject. The potential, therefore, of an endless production of heterogeneity from within the *poiesis* of the computational machine and its derivative architecture has the promise of actuating subjectivization as a product of architecture, as a productive affect. The production of singularities themselves are effects, whether of the built environment or of other origin, effects that might be termed following Deleuze and Guattari as "image-effects". The endless potential for the production of heterogeneity therefore is a promise fulfilled by a potential for subjectivization by way of unleashing image-effects of singularization, including in architecture. It is through this production that the politics of computational architecture and the promise of its inherent production of heterogeneity find the opportunity to play themselves out.

To quote Guattari in relation to the potential of architecture to forward and create such image-effects of singularization for the recreation of subjectivity and effect the process of subjectivization, we read his comments on Japanese architect Shin Takamatsu's work, that, "each element of the architectural ensemble (interior or exterior, and whatever its size), every ray of light, each possible shot [*prise de vue*] must therefore contribute to the total effect. [Machinic production] consists of passing from one register to another in order to set off an effect of de-centering the subject."[2] In the same essay Guattari writes, "The objective remains the same in each case: to arrive at a point where the building becomes a nonhuman subject, one which is capable of working with segments of both individual and collective subjectivities."[3] We read in these quotes the potential of architecture – whether digital or not – to fulfill a promise of creating and recreating subjectivity, of entering into a process of subjectivization of the users through a creation of effects of singularities. It is this relation and this process, or rather potential of architecture, which makes it a machine for heterogeneity, a machine for subjectivization; and it is this potential that might serve best as a model for its politics.

To quote Simone Brott from her book titled *Architecture for a free Subjectivity*, where she discusses Guattari's relation to specific architecture and his inter-relation of the creation of singularities and subjectivization vis-à-vis and by way of architecture, it is the production of singularities that:

> ...tackle the last frontier of the ascendant neo-liberal worldview; that is the frontier of "*what constitutes a subject?*" The evacuation [...] of such questions by the neo-Darwinian, deterministic forms of architecture based on Deleuze minus the subject (digital formalism, etc) make all the more pressing the resolution of the enterprise started by Guattari's inquest of architectural subjectivisation.[4]

Such architectural subjectivization is found within the creation of immanent impersonal effects, or in other terms the unleashing of image-effects through the inherent production of singularities by way of heterogeneity. Such a stance and politics is more than just the mere creation of form or surface, it is one of investing that form and surface with meaning, with communication, with a potential for heterogeneous image-effects to be unleashed in relation to use and function.

The promise of the computational politics of architecture through its production of heterogeneity is located thus in the production of singularities, of just such impersonal effects or image-effects being produced. Such a question is of an entirely different nature than the pursuit of a style or formalism, to which much computational architecture has attritioned into, but a possibility and promise of a politics of immanence within architectural production. It is by way of the production of "singularities", immanent impersonal affects or image-effects in our architecture that heterogeneity in its impact on subjectivization has the possibility to emerge. It is the promise of this possibility and the promise of such politics leading to it that is the promise for all architecture, whether computational or not.

The promise of the politics of digital architecture is thus its potential (not always and necessarily, or rather rarely fulfilled) of the production of singularities in users of it through infusing function and form with image-effects, and with it the production of new subjectivities in relation to those functions and forms. As Simone Brott has written in her above quoted book, the question that the politics of digital architecture must answer is:

How can we imagine an architecture irreducible to formalism, style, or rote instrumentality? [...] how can we create arrangements that come before the hijacking of territories and the typo-logics of pure forms? Or in other words, how can we rethink the "barbarity" of architectural identity and the "becoming" of architectural form? How do we make an architecture without qualities, erasing socio-economic and humanist forms of subjectivity and subjection?[5]

These pertinent questions might be followed on by quoting Jane Rendell: "In a world that currently remains in the grips of an unjust corporate and imperialistic capitalism, critical architecture is urgently required"[6] – or to paraphrase, in a world in which unjust and corporate imperialistic capitalism is often radically being questioned and attacked, just what kind of response can architecture muster?

It is in answer to these questions, and only to these questions, that the production of heterogeneity in and by way of singularities in the subject as the politics of digital architecture has promise. Such a question of politics begets the questions: just what kind of new worlds can architecture (our architecture) create and enact? What kind of new subjectivities might it lend itself to produce? What new thoughts and feelings might it engender in those who use it, whether that use is within the context of work or otherwise? In short, just what kind of effects might computational architecture see to produce? It is in engaging with and answering productively the possibility contained in these questions that the politics of digital architecture has the hope to play itself out, and has the hope of affecting a different kind of order in our cities and beyond, taking up and conjoining with the potential of our time and delivering on its promise.

As to the reason for this polemic, for the infusing of digital architecture making with heterogeneous image-effects for the promise of the production of altered subjectivities, for the creation of different subjectivization in users of architecture through its various functions and form, we might quote Félix Guattari: "The only acceptable end result of human activity is the production of subjectivity such that its relation to the world is sustained and enriched."[7] Thus Guattari gives us a model for any and all meaningful action, including that of the making of architecture, which is nothing other than the production of subjectivity in such a way as to enrich people's lives and their relation to the world and its everyday. Such a stance is a political one, a project that deliberately and consciously takes on making as a potential vehicle for otherness, and digital architecture production should not excuse itself from such rationale. Such production of subjectivity – whether through architecture or not – is what Guattari calls an "advancement of a new art of living"[8], of an altered way to relate to the everyday and to capitalist modes of subjectivization, and through that to life.

The creation and putting to use, the activating of singularities can take shape on and through any and all aspects of use of architecture and the built environment. It is achieved through the way subjectivity is formed or reformed, the way subjectivization occurs as a result of attributing function. The most basic premise to which such renewal of subjectivization and an advancement of a new art of living can be put to use might be found in the world of work – that is to create a different and other perception of work and relation to work through the singularities that create affect in the built environment of the workplace. Such a stance is not whether architecture put together in this vein might eliminate work, but rather how might it change subjects' relation to work and the workplace.

In examining the functional premise of work more closely in relation to the creation of different subjectivities in relation to it, we might assert following Foucault, that the function of work is related to history, to the historical process of humanity, and will only cease when that history terminates. To quote Foucault:

The great work of world history is inescapably accompanied by an absence of work, renewed at every moment but running on unaltered in its inevitable void throughout history; before history, since it is already there in the primitive decision, and after it again, since it will triumph with the last word that history pronounces."[9]

Likewise to any and all other production, architecture and its existence are also tied to this historical process as work, and with it to work as such. The question is how might architects create an affective environment of work-function, and in the process become agents of a political and historical process, especially in the context by which capitalism frames work. The mere form and surface finding of digital architecture's formalism and style needs to be made political and with it historical if it is to avoid descending further into a servitude of the spectacle, and it can achieve this by harnessing its making for the production of heterogeneous singularities in relation to functions such as work, in addition to any and all other subjectivizations life in capitalism faces. This is a question of making politics, of making architecture political, of activating the potential and promise of digital architecture as a historical construct and thus as a political one.

In returning to Foucault's quote earlier, we read that "work" as a phenomenon is tied to history, and with it to a particular action and process, that "work" arose at the time history arose, with work not having yet come into being before historical time, and to which absence of work we will return at the end of history. If digital architecture is to become a political agent that aims and hopes to challenge the status quo of our spectacle culture as opposed to being captured by it, if it aims to imbue its users with different ways of thinking, feeling and subjectivization, if it is thus to become truly political, and with it historical, forwarding a new art of living for which it has promise, the question is not the utopian one of initiating somehow "the end of work", but rather one of raising a different way of feeling and thinking about work and production, and with it history.

The raising to thought (and to arms) the imperative of a

different subjectivization in relation to work (to remain but at this example of function), of whether a potential politics of computational architecture, that is its *poeisis*, might bring about such difference, is tied to digital architecture's role in and on history as a historical and hence political product. If it is to truly become a historical and, by way of that, a critical mode of production, it must involve itself in its potential and promise of creating singularities in and through its built environment for the purpose of advancing heterogeneity. In doing so, the production of singularities and impersonal effects, that is the production of subjectivity and of difference within and through the production of architecture will most definitely, if employed, *change* subjectivity within the affects of the built environment given over to the function of work – and other everyday functions as well. It is the production of a change in subjectivity in relation to work and a certain subjectivization of work to which the production of singularities lends itself to, amongst many other everyday functions and actions. In as far as a different way to subjectivization in relation to work within the work environment and in the broader built environment and its everyday functions is achieved, the politics of a digital architecture fulfils a way toward its promise.

A Reading of Planonemons

The following essay will attempt to discuss the results of a particular encounter between philosophy and architecture exemplified in a collaboration between the architect Peter Eisenman and the philosopher Jacques Derrida to develop a garden scheme for the Parc de la Villette public works project in Paris.

The Eisenman-Derrida garden scheme at the Parc de La Villette was significant for the reason that it was the first acknowledged juncture by its participants in the modern oeuvre of architecture where philosophy was called on to interrogate the architectural process of form production. As a result of a collaboration taking place through and between philosophy and the production of an architectonic, possibilities opened up for discussing and acting on the relationship between philosophy and architectural production.

By way of reference, in the chapter "The Plane of Immanence" in Deleuze and Guattari's *What is Philosophy?*, philosophy is analogized with the ocean, where the fluctuation of the ocean gives rise to waves that move in a response to one another. These waves or forces are identified with philosophical concepts that are back-dropped against an underlying plane of immanence. In turn, this plane of immanence is constituted by a multiplicity of concepts that move at differing speeds and intensity to produce the very concepts in question that construct the plane. As such, philosophy is conceptualized as a series of interacting concepts operating against a foreground of their respective plane of immanence, an understanding that juxtaposes concept and plane into parallel phenomena, understanding them to operate in a reciprocal whole with the invention of the plane putting in place the phenomena of the planemonon from which concepts are created[1]. In other words, philosophical concepts reside as part of the plane of thought, and the plane of thought or concern of thought is seen as a horizon that is populated in turn by concepts to make it work and produce thought reciprocally.

Such structure of reciprocal registering is termed to be a "planonemon", whose working parts are seen as "abstract machines" giving rise to finite concepts[2]. This description is to say that the "abstract machine" precedes physicality and form; that is that it acts as a vector agent, gathering up disparate points as origins and articulating these points in its trajectory of movement and excretion. The abstract machine operates as a pre-formal diagram that lets loose creation into physicality and form; it multiplies the multiplicity of its origin into a physicality of form. The abstract machine thus becomes a function for thinking, made up of points and energized in flight from the sustenance of a plane of immanence.

The resultant architectonic of the collaboration for Eisenman and Derrida's garden scheme at Parc de la Villette can be seen to be a product of Deleuze's so-called "abstract machine", a philosophical concept concerned with production. It is through drawing on Deleuzian thought and terminology such as the concept of the "abstract machine" and related concepts, that Eisenman can be understood in part – as it will be argued – to instantiate the inter-relationship between philosophy and architecture.

From an understanding of this description, it should be asked what is the plane of immanence in operation in the Parc de La Villette garden scheme collaboration and what concepts or abstract machines are generated from this plane of immanence to let loose thinking and then subsequent production? That is, what is the mark of philosophy in the collaboration in question as an *apriori* to architectural physicality and form? Furthermore, once the abstract machines in question can be identified, it must be asked in what manner does this affect the formal outcome of architectural thinking in the project and give rise to form. The analysis of such an operation of this model in the Derrida-Eisenman garden scheme collaboration will shed light on the nature to which philosophy coupled with architecture to produce the possibility of form, and the extent to which the collaboration was fruitful.

To answer these questions, a detour back into Eisenman's formative architectural process must be had. The central concern of Eisenman's thinking in relation to architectural production throughout his practice has been an incessant analysis of the classical condition, more precisely a rigorous questioning directed toward the breaking down or tearing away from classical notions of representation in architecture in order to pursue the thought of modernity that is obscured by it. This pursuit has been articulated in his writing by way of rethinking the possibilities of the position of modernist thought in regards to the possibilities of architectural production. As far as this rigor in his thinking may be granted to him, it corresponds with Derrida's call, to go after architecture "not in order to attack, destroy or reroute it, to criticize or disqualify it. Rather in order to think it in fact, to detach itself sufficiently to apprehend it in a thought which goes beyond the theorem – and becomes a work in its turn"[3].

Eisenman's pursuit in going after the classical has been to deconstruct architecture, or "to think it in fact... to become a work in its turn". The process present in Eisenman's thinking on architecture resides upon a plane of deconstruction as a plane of immanence, an operation concerned with breaking down the condition and hegemony of the classical, in order to "not repress, but to surgically open up the classical [for the purposes of locating the] modern, and [thus] to find what is repressed"[4].

This pursuit of the deconstruction of the classical in Eisenman's architectural writings and thinking has operated as a means toward opening up the articulation and production of the metaphysics of architecture[5]. Metaphysics in architecture is to be understood as architecture's structure of appropriation of presence, order and unity, concepts that arise from Vitruvian thinking on firmness, utility and beauty. According to Eisenman and in contradistinction to the tradition of the metaphysics of architectural representation, architecture should be practiced and thought about as a continuous pursuit of the invention of dwelling[6]. For Eisenman, this pursuit is one of dislocating dwelling from the classical in order to rethink architecture for the possibility of a present modernity.

In articulating the metaphysics of architecture, Eisenman repeatedly sets into question notions surrounding the concepts of absence and presence coupled with the concepts of origin and destination or closure. In so doing, Eisenman articulates the concept of absence in an opposition to the practice of classicist representation. The classical representation of utility, firmness and beauty – for Eisenman – forms a closed order of architecture that is based upon an anthropocentric model of the cosmos and civilization. For Eisenman, such representation is seen as hegemonic of presence that is the representation of classicist figuration of an anthropocentric reality.

In his essay titled "Architecture and the Problem of the Rhetorical Figure", Eisenman equates presence with the act of representation naming the aesthetic of the object or the object's representation as the dominant form of presence[7]. To counter the hegemony of representation in architecture, Eisenman has argued for a strategy of absence, a contradistinction to presence, and in doing so attempts to set up an opposition between the representational and the rhetorical, saying that, "a representational figure represents a thing in its absence, a "Rhetorical figure" contains its absence, that is, it contains its open-endedness"[8]. Through this argument of the "Rhetorical figure", texts acting as a process for thinking offering another possibility for architecture are introduced into his work in general, and into his collaborative work with Derrida on the Parc de la Villette garden scheme in particular.

It is this deferral of the architectural to the textual that marks the point of infolding or engagement of the possibilities of philosophy in architecture. What is articulated in the use of the "Rhetorical figure" is a movement away from representation into a figuration of superimposition of several layers of *text* operating in simultaneity; it is thus that Eisenman attempts to move his thinking away from the classicist problem in architecture of origin, presence and ultimately the problem of representation.

In relation to origin – and its counter concepts of destination or closure – it is also through the "Rhetorical figure" as opposed to the "representational figure" that Eisenman argues that open-endedness can be achieved. This open-endedness is produced through incorporating super-positions into the design process. According to Eisenman, super-positions imposed on a site "result in a dislocation of origin and destination of time and space"[9]. Eisenman states that, "by incorporating in any site the assemblage from disparate but analogous elements of other sites, the two figures occupy origin and destination contemporaneously"[10] and therefore could be argued that they dislocate origin and presence in architectural composition.

The deconstruction of classical notions of representation and assemblage rely on just such mechanics that Eisenman calls the "Rhetorical figure". As such, the "Rhetorical figure" begins to act as an abstract machine before physicality and form are articulated or thought about. What the "Rhetorical figure" actually is in each case, or specifically in the case of the garden scheme for Parc de la Villette, is not yet of importance, merely its identification as a concept.

As Deleuze states in *What is Philosophy?*, "philosophy begins with the creation of concepts"[11], and so too does Eisenman's attempt at folding philosophy into the architectural process of form conception. What is found therefore in Eisenman's articulation of the "Rhetorical figure" as a tool for dislocating the thinking and production of architecture, is a point where philosophy becomes conversant with architecture and architecture becomes arrested, apprehended in thought in order to go beyond the theorem and become as such a work in its own turn, a result of its own cause.

Deleuze and Guattari write in their *What is Philosophy?* that "elements of the plane (of immanence) are *diagrammatic* features, whereas concepts are intensive features. Concepts are *intensive* and are therefore events"[12]. The "Rhetorical figure" in Eisenman's thinking is what Deleuze calls an intensive feature or concept that gives rise to an event, that is in architecture's case an event of physicality and form that results in some form of resolution of built form and space. In turn, the terms of absence, presence, origin and destination act as diagrammatic features, elements of a plane of immanence. The "Rhetorical figure" for Eisenman thus becomes a vector, carrying diagrammatic points of origin of thought in matter and function to excrete itself upon or within physicality and form. The "Rhetorical figure" is but one concept in operation in Eisenman's collaboration with Derrida.

In his essay "Moving Arrows, Eros and Other Errors", Eisenman discusses another process that when applied, similarly deconstructs origin and presence. Here, too, Eisenman deconstructs the anthropocentric principles of origin and presence found in classicist architecture to arrive at a process called "scaling". In Eisenman's essay "Moving Arrows, Eros and Other Errors", scaling can be identified with three terms that act as abstract machines. The abstract machines that can be identified as such operating in scaling are articulated thus: "scaling... proposes three destabilizing agents: discontinuity, which confronts the metaphysics of presence; recursivity, which confronts origin; and self-similarity, which confronts representation and the aesthetic object"[13]. The terms of "discontinuity", "recursivity" and "self-similarity" act as diagrammatic features or abstract machines that give rise to Eisenman's process called "scaling". Eisenman states, that the terms "discontinuity", "recursivity" and "self-similarity", "confront presence, origin and the aesthetic object in three aspects of the architectural discourse: site, programme and representation"[14]. What is seen in this statement is the relationship between the abstract machine operating in matter and function prior to physicality and presence, and the concept which operates on the plane of an event, which is to say in physicality and form (presence). Discontinuity, recursivity and self-similarity operate prior to site, program and representation and can thus be identified as abstract machines according to Deleuze and Guattari's *What is Philosophy?*, and an element of infusing the tectonic with the philosophical.

What thus can be seen in Eisenman's process, is a plane of immanence that gives rise to movement that rethinks or deconstructs the classicist notions of "origin", "presence", "discontinuity", "destination", "closure", "recursivity" and "self similarity" and in doing so gives rise to form in *apriori* to physicality. These terms can be seen as diagrammatic abstract machines or as a wave of the plane of immanence that gives rise to or animates other waves, waves that are intensive and coagulate in actively intensive precepts from where physicality and form might be sought. It is this operation that is evident in the manner by which philosophy attempted to couple with architecture to bring about something physical in the Parc de la Villette scheme. It is these concepts and the manner of their working or coming into being that are at the fore in Eisenman's collaboration with Derrida.

In the record of Eisenman and Derrida's first transcript of their collaboration, Eisenman initiates the participants to "construct a philosophical program for the collaboration"[15]. From the very outset, Eisenman's interest is focused on the possibilities of the philosophical in architecture in the act of engendering a space that opens up from between philosophy and architecture, which is to say from the textual as opposed to the representational. Later in the same transcript, after Eisenman has presented his ongoing interests in deconstructing anthropocentric representation in architecture and the response elicited from Derrida to this in describing a passage on *Chora* from Plato's Timeaus, Eisenman goes on to say that, "I don't care if we make a garden or not. I mean, after all, there are any number of gardens. We should try to find a program for the presence of the absence of *Chora* and concentrate on making that sensible"[16].

Thus, what is set up in the collaboration is the search for a vector-based agent or abstract machine through which something sensible might be generated, namely the physical representation of *Chora*. This model of operation is none-other than an attempt at bleeding architecture open to the philosophical, of allowing the philosophical (textual) to penetrate the corpse of architecture and implant or graft onto it something that derives its origin from a philosophical plane of immanence as opposed to a representational image. The task in concentrating on "making something sensible" is the setting in motion of an abstract machine that might generate features that excrete physicality and form. Hence, the collaboration becomes a vehicle for the infolding of architecture and philosophy onto one another: to collapse philosophy into the sensible realm of form, or in Eisenman's words, "How does one turn Jacques Derrida into a synthesizer? How does one make him make?"[17] – or in other terms, how does one produce "*tekton*" out of philosophy?

In elucidating a response from Derrida on Eisenman's interest in the concepts of absence, origin and presence, Derrida reiterates his suggestion from an essay draft that he had been writing at the time, involving a piece of text from Plato's *Timeaus*. The text in question is a fictional record of a dialogue between Plato and Socrates on the concept of "place". The name attributed to this place in the text is the aforementioned "*Chora*". Derrida goes on to explain, that the concept of *Chora* is a fictional invention that exists on the one hand outside the intelligent realm of *eidos* and on the other, aside from *eidos'* inscription of the sensible in the realm of time. This third state, or *"triton genos"* as Derrida calls it, is a place in which everything, both the intelligent eternal realm of *eidos* and the time-based realm of the sensible, is imprinted.

Thus *Chora* receives everything, it is where everything takes place, yet no imprint remains on it. It acts as a virgin place, one in which both the realm of *eidos* and the realm of the sensible are absent: a place for giving and receiving; unintelligible for the intelligent and un-representable in the sensible. As such it is a fictional non-place whilst actually being a philosophical place, at the same time impossible to be brought into the sensible since it can not be made: a third place aside or in extra to the intelligent *eidos* and the sensible space-time matter. "The moment one attempts to comprehend it, to define it, one reduces its value because it can not be defined"[18]; as such it can also not be represented.

As the discussion ensues, Eisenman lunges for the description of the concept of *Chora* as precisely what seems to lend itself to the possibility of deconstructing origin, presence and absence. However, since *Chora* can not be represented because it exists outside the intelligent realm of *eidos* as well as that of sensible space-time material representation, he makes the suggestion that the project attempt to represent the absence of *Chora*, the presence of the absence or the structure of the absence of *Chora*[19]. As such, the concept of *Chora* or rather the concept of the absence of *Chora* becomes a vehicle for the possibilities of the architec-tonic of presence and absence, a philosophical deconstruction of classicist origin.

What is being sought in this discussion of the concept *Chora* and the transcript to follow is a programmatic structure through which a burden of origin and accompanying presence can be evaded. By suspending the hierarchy of Vitruvian order and its accompanying hegemony of utility, firmness and beauty, origin and presence for architecture can be sought in something other. In fact, Eisenman's concern as discussed in his essay "The End of the Classical: the End of the Beginning, the End of the End" and in the previously quoted "Architecture and the Problem of the Rhetorical Figure" is to allude or extinguish origin and presence in architecture altogether, to posit architecture onto a schema of thinking that through such extinguishment bypasses presence in architecture and thus origin. It is in evading a classicist notion of presence and origin that the architecture of absence or a modernist deconstruction in Eisenman's view can be formulated.

What is suggested by Eisenman from the conclusion of this initial collaborative discussion, is a series of texts that superimposed on one another destabilize any reference to origin and thus of presence. A suggestion is made to work with Plato's text on *Chora*, superimposed by Derrida's text on Plato and a third text to be written by Eisenman on Plato's text on *Chora* and Derrida's text on Plato. What is being sought to be set up is a fictional textual-come-programmatic space that acts as a receptacle to three layers of thought and by doing so eludes origin, akin to the concept named the "Rhetorical figure". The information registered on the site in response to such a program would be an "analogic structure of registration"[20]. It is from inside this analogic structure of registration that information on the structure of a deconstructed architectonic would be provided for: that is the concept of the "Rhetorical figure" be activated to produce physicality and form – that is a percept – which evades an origin, that is exists outside any origin of a reference, thus attempting to constitute a non-representational loop.

The textual layers of the program come to act as a concept articulated by the name "Rhetorical figure". This concept of the "Rhetorical figure" as a programmatic function comes to articulate and interact with the concept of *Chora*. So we have two concepts that interact with one another in hope or promise of creating the physical.

Deleuze discusses the term concept in *What is Philosophy?* as a creation that "does not have spatio-temporal coordinates only intensive ordinates"[21], which is to say, that the concept in itself is not a physical formulation and can never be so, but rather creates intensities by which physicality might be produced. Hence a bridge is required through which the concept, or namely the concept of the "Rhetorical figure" and through it the concept of *Chora* might be given representational form – if that is at all possible.

In the third transcript of the collaboration, discussion turns to the way in which this de-centered, origin-evacuating textual program might be realized in physicality. A number of metaphors are produced in the discussion in order to situate the manner by which the programmatic considerations might be able to be activated. The three metaphors used are the "quarry", the "palimpsest" and the "labyrinth"[22].

The "quarry" is suggestive of a place where origin has been erased from and thus operates as a metaphor for erasure. The "palimpsest" becomes a vehicle for dislocating origin, and is harnessed in order to superimpose Bernard Tschumi's plan for La Villette over the archaeology of La Villette, thus eluding an origin of the site. The "labyrinth" is suggested as a tool for deconstructing the narrative or the continuousness of the program, and as such it is intended to activate the evacuation of presence.

The three metaphors therefore are harnessed for the programmatic activation of erasure, the dislocation of origin and the evacuation of presence. These three metaphors can be considered to be the articulation of events that the concept of *Chora* and the concept of the "Rhetorical figure" has set into being. The question that must be asked, however, is what happens at the point of the concept becoming metaphor? Is something lost in the philosophical, is it the only way in which a bridge can be constructed for philosophy to intermingle with an architectonic of architecture?

In order to examine the question of the metaphor in relation to the philosophical and its intended pro-genitive in this project, that is the physical, Deleuze writes that, "philosophy proceeds with sentences, but it is not always propositions that are extracted from sentences in general"[23]. In the case of the collaboration, what is extracted from philosophy's proceeding are metaphors that act as propositions for the physical, as quasi linguistic prototypes for what is to be realized. Deleuze states further, that, "from sentences or their equivalent, philosophy extracts concepts... and art extracts percepts and affects"[24]. So what is found to be extracted in the collaboration is a set of concepts, namely *Chora* and the "Rhetorical figure", and a set of percepts or affects that are articulated through the use of metaphors.

A question in the process of extraction of philosophy must, however, be asked: what is the relation in the case at hand between the concept of *Chora* and the percepts of the quarry, palimpsest and the labyrinth? Deleuze provides a suggestion to this question by paralleling the percepts and the concepts back to the substance of philosophy that is language: "In each case language is tested and used in incomparable ways – but in ways that do not define the difference between disciplines without also constituting their perpetual interbreeding"[25]. What happens at the point of sentences or philosophy becoming metaphor, is a constitution of "perpetual interbreeding" between philosophy and architecture, an interbreeding that "does not define the difference between its disciplines"[26]. What thus results through the use of concepts come metaphors in this collaboration is on the one hand the application of the concepts of *Chora* and the "Rhetorical figure", and on the other a set of percepts and affects identified by the metaphors as derivative of them, that have resulted from the concepts interbreeding with an other discipline, namely the burden of the architectural of having to build something physical.

At the point of the instituting of metaphors for the production of the physical, what we find is that philosophy or language becomes folded onto or grafted into as an alien seeking a new home in architecture. This graft of philosophy onto architecture provides the value and purpose of the project and it is in this act of grafting that the collaboration could be seen to have some legitimacy.

It may be questioned, however, whether what is being conducted in this collaboration can be called to be philosophy at all? Deleuze suggests that, "the object of philosophy is to create concepts that are always new"[26]. The collaboration achieves in creating concepts that suggest another way for constructing architecture that deliver on eluding the confines of classicist representation; whether that is new in the sense of thought is indeterminable, as it comes about in physicality. The concept of *Chora* becomes "the contour, the configuration, the constellation of an event to come"[27]. Furthermore, Deleuze states that, "those who do not renew the image of thought are not philosophers but functionaries..."[28] It might be said that this could be achieved through the deconstruction of representation, origin and absence – the components of the concept of *Chora* – in the setting up of the programmatic textual-come-metaphorical layers. The metaphors then would act as images of thought, renewed images of thought that act as a graft of implanting the physical reality of building with philosophical discourse and thus attain to renewing the image of thought as philosophy in a physically built form as outcome. It must be noted however, that with this strategy not only is philosophy hoped to be created, but also and with it the renewing of the image of the architectural.

Once the metaphors are derived from the philosophical, that is the tools that graft the philosophical into the physical are instituted, it should be understood what the philosophical is and how it works. This is important in order to understand the nature of the philosophical in relation to the concrete act of making something in form. It is this direction of thinking and presupposition which is the purpose and rationale of the collaboration after all.

What is important to us in such an understanding of Deleuze's structure of philosophy, is first of all from what plane of thought the collaboration is working from, that is what is immanent to it and secondly how this plane gives way to concepts, that is intensive features or intentions that activate the process of forming an architectonic. It might be suggested that the plane of immanence that has been instituted in the collaboration is an intuition concerned with deconstructing a classicist origin and presence in representation – a deconstruction of the hegemony of classicism. The immanence of this plane gives rise to the introduction of the concept of *Chora*, a borrowed concept that carries with it a possibility for an event of physicality in the form of representing its absence. This absence of the concept of *Chora* is attempted to be realized in the collaboration by setting up a system of metaphors that allow a grafting to occur between the philosophical nature of the concept and the physical demands of architecture. The metaphors come about from a different form of extraction. It is at this point in the collaboration, that a new device or process is introduced derived from the metaphors of quarry, palimpsest and labyrinth that allow for the identification or actualization of an architectonic scheme. This introduced process is, as mentioned before, called scaling.

The process of scaling is a non-philosophical process or tool harnessed to transform the graft of the metaphors into built reality. It is at this point that the collaboration and design process departs from the philosophical and enters the purely material. What happens from this point on in the collaboration is a movement away from the shared zone of philosophy-architecture that existed at the point of the metaphors being derived from the absence of the concept of *Chora*. The metaphors share in both the philosophical and in the promise of the architecture as realized form to follow. The process of scaling, however, moves the metaphors away from the philosophical toward the realm of building. It can be argued how seamless this transition actually is, and whether the process of scaling can be attributed to be derived from the realm of the concept, which is to say philosophy, or whether it exists apart from it.

What happens in the process of scaling in this scheme, is the setting up of four superimposed sites/projects, namely that of the site of Parc de la Villette itself, Tschumi's grid project for this park[29], the site of Cannaregio – a theoretical project Peter Eisenman worked on in Venice[30], and the project that Peter Eisenman did for the Cannaregio site also utilizing a grid super-imposition. These four sites/projects all using a rectilinear grid system are superimposed vertically on one another at different scales in such a way to notate different times – past, present and future – of the projects/sites and the different conditions of solid and void as form and receptacle present in them.[31] What this scaling diagram sets out to achieve, is to construct a series of solid and void permutations that circumvent the condition of origin and presence by referring to another place and another time. In this way, what presents itself in the garden – the archi-tectonic of the scheme – is held to elude figurative representation and to become a receptacle of time and scale: past, present and future and the various differing scales of each superimposed project/site. The representation of origin and absence becomes a derivation of superimposed projects and sites at different scales and moments, which deliver presence or the architectonic of the site into an abstract non-figurative condition. It is in this way that the absence of the concept of *Chora* is hoped to be materialized.

In order to destabilize the hierarchical closed loop set up by the site/projects in the process of scaling, a mark or drawing is solicited by Eisenman from Derrida that would be incorporated into the project in order to break the totalizing hierarchy of the scaling process. It is intended that this piece be a heterogeneous piece that is impossible to integrate into the scheme, thus breaking the circle of relationship between the palimpsest, quarry and labyrinth appropriation of scaling.[32] What is suggested by Derrida, is a metallic gold object or sculpture in the form of a grid sieve or lyre, representing the choral work of the collaboration. An object that is at once alien from the project – thus affecting a discontinuity that opens up the work to other readings – but also representative of Plato's text on *Chora*. It is by instituting this piece onto the site, that a deferral from the present-past, past-future presence of voids and presences is hoped to be achieved. Through this de-totalizing sieve or lyre sculpture, a relationship is hoped to be set up with what Derrida calls in the transcripts of the collaboration an ur-future and/or ur-memory that destabilizes the project from a system of closed representation, and opens it up to further readings constructed by the user-thinker-public.

A trajectory of philosophy coupling with architecture is thus seemed to be set up. This trajectory has its origin in language and text, and its outcome in physicality and form. In reality, the movement of this trajectory is one of extracting from the philosophical something that can be represented and thus built. It is in the hinge between the philosophical and the representational that the problems of a marriage between philosophy and architecture can be found. Whether this bridge was crossed from within the possibilities of operation of the philosophical, or whether it was removed through the introduction of scaling from philosophy's possibility of playing itself out, is the moment of problematisation and the place of critique of the ultimate value of the collaboration's objectives.

In his essay "Why Eisenman Writes Such Good Books", Derrida analyses the results of the collaboration, the moments of truth, of discontinuity and fault lines in the collaboration and comments on Eisenman's preoccupation with language, which directed and instituted the collaboration of the garden.

In a somewhat ironic tone, Derrida comes to a conclusion that Eisenman's preoccupation with language operates on an appropriation of readings and word-plays into slippages of meanings, and from within these slippages finds a way to affect an architectonic articulation: "Eisenman not only takes great pleasure, jubilation, in playing with language, with languages, at the meeting of many idioms, welcoming chances, attentive to the *alea*, to transplants, to the slippings and derivations of the letter. He takes this play seriously..."[33] Perhaps this is what was at play in the naming of the metaphors. Can such an approach to language and to text, however, amount to anything philosophical, or is it just a misappropriation of discourse? Is the play of philosophy played out through a lunging at language's twists and turns, and is what is fabricated from those twists and turns faithful to the trajectory and promise of a meeting between philosophy and architecture? Derrida's comments on the collaboration in "Why Eisenman Writes Such Good Books" is, however, a comment on the collaboration and how it proceeded rather than on the promise or possibility of philosophy infolding into architecture per say.

In order to establish the validity of the collaboration in light of the philosophical graft, Eisenman offers us the following thought from his essay "The End of the Classical" from which this might be measured: "Since any process must necessarily have a beginning and a movement, however, the fictional origin must be considered as having at least a methodological value – a value concerned with generating the internal relations of the process"[34]. The fictional origin of Eisenman's collaboration with Derrida is the graft of the absence of the concept of *Chora*, the fiction of *Chora* into the architectural process of generating architectonic form.

This concept, and the percepts and affects that were extracted from it, underwent a process of "scaling" that acted as a bridge between the philosophical and the architectonic. It must be asked, however, what is the value of this process in light of the "internal relations" of philosophy itself, which is the origin, be it fictional or otherwise, of the movement and process of the collaboration?

Through understanding, or at least discussing the internal relations of philosophy itself, of how philosophy proceeds, a measurement of the methodological process of "scaling" can be evaluated and a proper perspective gained on the validity of the outcome of the collaboration. For what is at stake here, is the internal relations of philosophy itself and whether the promise of the graft of philosophy played itself out on the architectonic, thus validating a meeting between philosophy and architecture and the collaboration between Eisenman and Derrida.

Deleuze discusses the nature of philosophy, art and science as three distinct planes that have their own internal method of production.

> For philosophy, this method proceeds through laying out a plane of immanence and creating concepts upon that plane that the conceptual personae constructs. For art, the plane becomes a plane of composition from which percepts and affects or sensations are affected. In the case of philosophy, the creation of concepts proceeds through conceptual personae, in the case of art (or for this argument architecture, that is in this case a compositional art) the composition of sensations or a reading proceeds through "aesthetic figures"[35].

These two figures, the conceptual personae and the aesthetic figure operate on two distinct planes, one on a plane of immanence, the other on a plane of composition. What these two activities of creation and composition have in common is their relationship to the infinite, to what Deleuze calls "chaos":

> ...philosophy wants to save the infinite by giving it consis-
> tency: it lays out a plane of immanence that, through the
> action of conceptual personae, takes events or consistent
> concepts to infinity [...] art wants to create the finite that
> restores the infinite: it lays out a plane of composition that, in
> turn, through the action of aesthetic figures, bears
> monuments or composite sensations[36].

It is these "composite sensations" that Eisenman wanted to affect
as a reading of different times and sites, or in other terms, a
reading of absence of origin, presence and representation. The
reading of Eisenman's "composite sensations" in the garden
scheme thus becomes a reading of fictions. It is these fictions that
are hoped to lead to a destabilizing of representation and with it
origin and figurative presence. What the question of the collaboration focuses around, however, is the reading of fictions as a
result of the creation and subsequent comprehension of the
concepts at play. A slippage is actively sought out between the
plane of immanence and its concepts and the plane of composition and its sensations. It is only through such a slippage being
successful, that the instituting of a fiction originating from a
plane of immanence might have the possibility to be activated in
the "monument" of sensations.

The method through which this might proceed is laid out in
Deleuze's final chapter of *What is Philosophy?* Prior to examining
the method by which the plane of immanence of philosophy and
the plane of composition of architecture might be able to
intersect, Deleuze suggests the following: "Abstract art seeks
only to refine sensation, to dematerialize it by setting out an
architectonic plane of composition in which it would become a
purely spiritual being, a radiant thinking and thought matter, no
longer sensation of see or tree, but a sensation of the concept of

sea or concept of tree"[37].

Herein lies the rationale and ultimate goal of Eisenman's collaboration with philosophy: to articulate or affect a reading of the architectonic that becomes, or is, a sensation of the concept of the absence of *Chora*. Not a singular reading as monument, but a multiple reading, each as to him/herself, a subliminal sensation of the absence of origin and the absence of presence.

It is at this point that the rationale of the process of scaling might seem to have its validity. For what Deleuze suggests, is that such a creation-affect, one that neither belongs to the realm of concept, but neither fully to the realm of percept or affect can only proceed through each disciplines own methods. This is the first "model" of inter-disciplinary interference that Deleuze articulates, namely that "...the rule is that the interfering discipline must proceed with its own methods"[38]. It is therefore necessary for a non-conceptual, non-philosophical process to make its mark. This mark is brought forth in the search for an architectonic, through the application of the "scaling" diagrams as a process that marks the outcome as architecture and delivers the sensation of the absence of the concept of *Chora* and the concept of the "Rhetorical figure" to the "reader".

Philosophy or the concepts of *Chora* and the "Rhetorical figure" and the resultant metaphors of quarry, palimpsest and labyrinth could not proceed in any other way to "create the finite that restores the infinite". Without the process of scaling, the collaboration would have descended back into chaos and no junction made between philosophy and architecture. What is paramount, however, is the efficacy of such a method. Without a "method" or process that extracts and posits sensation as a monument, and as an effective monument at that, such a process of grafting one discipline onto the other would be rendered meaningless.

Philosophy proceeds in its intersection with art, architecture or any other creative discipline through the promise of a method or process borrowed from that host discipline that enables concepts to be articulated into sensations. It is inside this switch or grafting method by which philosophy becomes animate in the creative or compositional arts and casts its shadow onto production and into physicality and form. The nature, structure and efficacy of this graft in order to be successful, must result from an invention that resides within the host discipline. To reiterate Eisenman, "to invent an architecture is to allow architecture to be a cause; in order for it to be a cause, it must arise from something outside a directed strategy of composition"[39]. It is the strength of that invention that delivers the promise of philosophy to production.

To conclude the examination of the collaboration in the light of philosophy's grafting of itself onto architecture, it must be articulated, that architecture remained precisely because of the process of scaling, its own internal method, on its own plane, utilizing its own elements[40]. Such an observation extinguishes the claim by critics of Eisenman's architecture, that what he is doing is not architecture. For what is seen from the above brief analysis is, that what he has done in the collaboration for a garden scheme at Parc de la Villette is precisely to remain on the plane of composition as Deleuze and Guattari elaborate it; an architectonic could not have been realized otherwise.

Arguably, in the scheme's architectonics' sensation or reading "concepts and sensations become undecidable, at the same time as philosophy and art become indiscernible, as if they shared the same shadow that extends itself across their different nature and constantly accompanies them"[41], thus writes Deleuze and Guattari on a possible efficacy of such inter-bleeding of disciplines. It is the casting of this shadow that renders philosophy and composition into an undecidable state evacuating in the case of the garden scheme architectonic the concerns of origin, presence and representation and through it deconstructing the hierarchy of the Vitruvian polemic. The conjoined shadow of differing disciplines was thus attempted to be extended across the architectonic in order for the different nature of philosophy and architecture to emerge as a singular reading of the infinite fulfilling the promise of their interference.

The Path on which Architecture Finds Itself

"Let us consider architectural thinking. By that I don't mean to conceive architecture as a technique separate from thought and therefore possibly suitable to represent it in space, to constitute almost an embodiment of thinking, but rather to raise the question of architecture as a possibility of thought, which cannot be reduced to the status of representation of thought."[1]

Jacques Derrida, Architecture, Where Desire May Live

This quote comes from the introduction of one of the late-Jacques Derrida's writings on architecture from the mid-1980s titled "Architecture, Where Desire May Live", written at a time and in a context when Derrida was engaged with reflecting on architecture philosophically. The intentional resurrection and resurfacing of this quote offers a possibility to re-interrogate, re-approach and think through what in fact architecture as a possibility of thought might be, and what substrates of life might go into its constitution, and by which it comes to exist. By resurrecting the thinking in this quote, such re-thinking and reflection might provide a theoretical speculation on the possibly hidden process involved in the making of place, taking possession of space and the conception of related built environments.

"Architecture as a possibility for thought", as Derrida raises his call, involves thinking through and attempting to answer the question as to what is actually the essence and substance of architecture, the architectural process and of built environments. In rephrasing this statement as a question we might ask: what is the most basic condition of process that lends itself to an activity that results in architecture? In answering this question we might hope to be able to approach "raising architecture to the possibility of thought" and to think through its substance.

In response to this question, the first implicit thread that might be surmised is that to think and raise architecture to thought requires the satisfaction and interrogation of two basic conceptual terms with which architecture is involved and which it can't escape in its reason of being, namely "placing" and "habitation". It is above all the essence contained in the activity denoted by these two terms that the master (*archi*) builder comes to construct (*tecture*) something that is a built environment: taking place resulting in a use for a type of habitation. How does the master constructor (architect) of placing and consequential habitation come to arrive at the outcomes of his/her action, resulting in the process of a "placing" taking place for the provision of "habitation"? It is in thinking through the genesis of these two terms that result in the possibility of raising architecture to thought.

Such outcome of a "placing" and resultant "habitation" have as their least, and even then only, peripheral prerequisite, the choice and subsequent use of site in the physical sense; the real substance of the terms "placing" and "habitation" are only revealed after it is examined how these processes come about, what lies behind these processes, or in other terms, what is the genesis of the activity denoted by these terms. It is this hidden origin latent within the activity of making architecture that offers up a possibility of displacement of usual ways of comprehending the architectural process, and in turn for revealing that which is hidden within it.

In "taking possession of place" a habitation is constructed, and in turn a "habitation" cannot proceed without a taking possession of place. The terms "placing" and "habitation" are thus mutually reliant on one another, and it is in this mutual reliance that architecture eventuates and takes its place. Habitation is thus a result of the taking possession of a space resulting in a place, and it is in the consequence of the creation of a place that architecture and a subsequent built environment can be, and is, articulated.

With the taking place of possession of space in which habitation comes about, a marking-out and articulation of a particular resultant environment is constructed, regardless of the nature, condition or resultant physicality of what might follow. This is to say, that a set of internal, pre-formed psychological metaphorical paths are activated that have been formed *apriori* in thought, which then come to constitute our taking possession of place and anything that might ensue. The taking possession of a place, which is to say the institution of a space *as* place and subsequent or consequent habitation in that place – and the resultant consideration of architecture as a possibility and housing for the making of that taking place – go hand-in-hand. It is impossible to think through either activity, or even to realize either activity, without thinking through both at the same time and in the context of the mental substance that the paths of our psychological content affect in and on a place and its taking possession of it. It is this condition of coagulation within us and between a resultant built environment that lead to the manifesting of a place. This is to say that it is in a manifestation of the psychological content of our mental paths in creating a place that the nature of architecture and the possibility to think an eventuating architecture is revealed. In the process of a habitation of a place being taken hold of, it is the psychological conditioning and content of our mental paths that construct the nature of what is revealed physically in that place: that is an architecture – an architecture created from the inside-out: the nature of architecture being constituted from our conscious and unconscious interior as it acts to take possession of space.

The interior psychological content of our mental paths that take possession of a space and that stamp themselves on a space to create place are affected by "us", what we may term, following Deleuze and Guattari, as *haecceity*, that is the "thisness" of a thing or person in its entire individuated aggregate[2]. It is our lines, our slownesses and speeds,[3] or in another term our "thisness" that causes us to create and follow particular lines of thought and consequent action and making; it is our interior, psychological – conscious or unconscious – lines, slownesses and speeds, our "thisness" that causes a space to be inhabited in a particular way, and by virtue of that to be reflected back as a place, be it physically built in its nature or otherwise; it is our individuated inner psychological aggregate that stamps possession on a space, creating a "thisness" or habitation, a possession that becomes a placing. The affect of creation of place is therefore an affect of us, the reflection of our entire individuated and collective aggregate. Habitation and the conscious or unconscious paths which lead to, in and through a making of a place once it is formed are a resultant creation and manifestation of our *haecceity*.

The substance denoted by the terms "placing" and "habitation" lead to suggesting an *apriori*, internal, pre-formed psychological set of metaphorical paths of disposition by which an activity of "placing" and consequential "habitation" is made and can be effected. It is in uncovering these *apriori* inner-psychological processes and highlighting them as the substance of any making of place and consequential nature of habitation where the thinking through and interrogation of architecture begins.

In reference to Bernard Tschumi's *Event Cities 3*, the creation of place may depart through three different approaches: context, concept and content.[4] What must be examined in unraveling the nature of psychological paths taken and affected in realizing architecture is the substance of each: the substance of the term "context", the substance of the term "concept" and the substance of the term "content".

To begin with the first term, Tschumi discusses in his introduction to *Event Cities 3* that "context" is defined in terms of that which is "in situ", a given historical, geographic, social, political or economic setting. Historical, geographic, social, political and economic contexts are already consequences of prior instances of taking place: they are the result of previous mental paths having been unraveled making a place. These previous outcomes of making place affect the condition and nature of our own subsequent place making *apriori*: we can only respond to them in some way, and therefore they affect any subsequent making of place whether we are aware of it or not.

The substance of "context" thus both precedes, and reciprocally in turn creates, variegated forms of subsequent taking possession of place, and with it any consequential architecture. Tschumi's ascribed attribute of a place in the term of "context" shapes our own subsequent mental paths of making place in that space; they impact as a consequence of a prior taking possession and taking place.

The second term related to taking possession of place, "concept", can be understood as the manifestation of an internal psychological assemblage of how we have been assembled in space and time and *as a result* of space and time, of how the spatiality of our epoch affects itself in the act of our own modes of habitation of space, of the affects of our epoch in and on us, prior to even setting out on any path that might create such habitation, and prior to an act of taking place.

The substance of the architectural term "concept" is thus affected by the coagulated formulation, or "thisness" of us in the world, our thoughts and desires as they have come to be constructed in and through the world, with the world reflecting itself back into a making place through us. This reflection might be construed as an intellectual or mental context of a life-world's reflection. The substance of refraction contained within the assemblage of the architectural concept being forwarded, in the taking possession of a space and the particular use, or putting to use, of a "context" that might ensue, is influenced by technology, society, politics, and/or a myriad other substrates that have come to form our epoch and in turn us, resulting in inflecting a particular way of consequential inhabiting.

The refractions found in a "concept" are the stamp of our inner paths, the corridors, passages, staircases and doors of our collective conscious and unconscious as informed by our epoch in the act of taking possession of space and creating place. As such it contains the motivation and the will that leads us on a particular path of taking possession of a space in a particular way and recreating it as a particular kind of place; it is a psychological fall-out that cannot but affect in space something that is a refraction of our *haecceity*, and with it, a refraction of the world. Refractions as "concepts" are constructed in our interior conscious or unconscious, which by default construct a placing for what is to come.

Taking possession of a space and making place in such under-standing is a matter of comprehending "creating place and habitation" as something that is first and foremost an interior emanation, an operation that works from the inside-out, rather than one constructed from outside-in as a result of something being first built and then experienced and used. The results and outcomes of creating place and consequent habitation, and hence the substantive nature of the condition of a resultant built environment and with it architecture, is therefore the result of an *apriori*, interior condition first and foremost, which becomes affected on the outside in a physical manner. It is this "affect of the internal", whether of "context" or "concept", which creates resultant "content" that is experienced in the course of habitation.

"Content" is the sum total of the outcome of "context" and "concept" once the taking possession of place has been executed, or rather revealed from a conscious/unconscious psychological internal milieu. The "content" of a place is the collective aggregate of the outcome of the intermingled lines of "context" and "concept" having come to pass and being experienced and used. It is the nature of a given "context", coupled by the nature of the resultant "concept" that creates a particular type of "content", and it is this outcome of "content" that defines the nature of a place and creates the place-making resulting in a particular type of habitation. The resultant "content" of a place comes into being from an internal coagulation of the maker(s) of that place, and as a result that space having been taken possession of in a particular way in line with the inner, mental workings of the maker (architect), whether something physical is built or not.

The substance of content that stamps its presence on all architectural and/or physical place-making is resultant from individuated and collective psychology as well as conscious and unconscious desire – that is us – our civilization and culture as we have come to be assembled by it and come to act from it. Place-making is thus – following Lyotard[5] – an outcome of our economy of libidinal investment, and following Deleuze and Guattari, our *haecceity*, it is something that exists *apriori* in our make-up, and comes to affect in a place's content once it has been made.

In clarifying these comments, the libidinal that is being talked about here is of Jung's libido of general psychical instincts or life drive, as opposed to Freud's libidinal of sexual drive. The making of place in this Jungian understanding is thus a revealing of our inner, psychological, conscious and unconscious constitution and psychical instincts as they come to bare upon space and taking possession of it. Such thinking concerning "place" and "making place", turns the accepted conception of the nature of place emanating from its physical qualities on its head, and rather aims to privilege and set in focus the hidden, psychical and psychological make-up of the process by which its makers are, or have been, assembled and who then come to act from that assemblage.

In extending this thinking to "raising architecture to a possibility of thought", it might be surmised that the crossroads that lead towards, and at which we find architecture creating place, and through which we can apprehend architecture as a possibility of thought, is the intersection of the substance of "context" and the substance of "concept" as internal, psychical phenomena. Before and prior to taking place, they are interior, that is to say psychological in their substantive nature.

The crossroads of "context" and "concept", the metaphorical path or street that leads us to a particular environment in which habitation takes place, that is its precondition, is that which forms our individuated and collective subjectivities. In thinking about place in such a way, one arrives at an understanding of "place", "taking possession of space" and "making place" as foremostly a conscious and/or unconscious emanation of the Jungian libido, a psychological process and outcome in its source. This is to say that the architectural process of making place is nothing else than an immanence of an already pre-existent condition of ourselves and our unconscious libidinal constitution that is already existent and assembled prior to habitation taking place or being articulated in a particular way.

Baudrillard says that his idea of architecture, "is that architecture starts from space, which is the primary scene, and that architecture fills it"[6], with architecture being "an empty matrix of interior space... capable of generating space instead of managing it."[7] This "empty matrix of interior space" should be thought of as everything that has come to form us in our individuated and collective aggregate, our own personal psychological structure as that which is formed by culture, society, civilization, education, our epoch and much more besides, which subsequently comes to expression in a physical architecture.

The path of taking possession of space and of creating architecture as a spatial construct thus has myriad lines of conscious and unconscious internal psychological content operating as its economy, which assemblage is placing's economy. It must be argued that both architecture's resultant content and the resultant place's nature reside in the economy of the libido. In order to reveal the nature of architecture and with it the nature of place, and offer it up as a possibility for thought, it is the substance of our interior formulation that requires to be thought through, and if necessary critiqued and challenged.

The path on which architecture finds itself and itself can in turn to be found, the implicit precondition for habitation and placing, of making place and the possibility for architecture to be thought, emanates from the formation of our individuated and collective psychology. It is first and foremost libidinal as it has come to construct us: as Derrida has titled his essay from which we began, an "Architecture: Where Desire May Live".

The importance, therefore, of our individual and collective unconscious and libidinous desire is the central seam and guiding substance to the condition of a resultant "place" in the outcome of its making. This is to argue that it is in an understanding of our own libidinal constitution that the path on which place, making place, taking possession of space, and hence architecture as place's operative tool finds itself.

In accepting this argument, the process of architecture in making place resides in an *apriori* condition of our libidinal-psychological construction as each might bare upon his/her practice in the internal construction and context of ourselves, and thus it is in this substance of "us", in our libidinal constitution that "making place" and any resultant built environment's outcome of "content" rests. What sort of place we might desire to make is rather a question of, "How are we psychologically assembled in our subjectivity by our societies, cultures, civilization and our epoch in relation to taking possession of space for a particular habitation?" It is this relation that determines any and all resultant architecture and built environment, and by which places have been, are and will be defined.

Questions Concerning the Redevelopment of Ground Zero

On the morning of 11 September 2001, a momentous event took place in New York and Washington, one that has since substantially come to define much of global politics, political discourse and action, including considerable aspects of foreign policy as well as internal politics of nation-states of the present and foreseeably of generations to come. This event, colloquially known and referred to as 9/11, has had an impact on questions as far ranging as emancipation, civil rights, women's rights, border control, immigration, and not least militarization, specifically in the context of international conventions and treatises spelled out by the charter of the United Nations on the ethics and legal use of pre-emptive military force, as well as inspiring painters, graphic artists, directors, actors, film-makers and composers in pursuit of artistic and cultural expression dealing with that eventful day. In examining the intellectual, political, cultural and artistic footprint and fall-out of the event of 9/11, exhaustive studies and work could be made in all these various disciplinary areas, and in many cases have indeed been made.

In raising the specter of thought for a moment beyond the most obvious areas of concern that have been effected and brought into play by the event of 9/11, a speculation on the nature and context of the event of 9/11 and its resultant horizons cannot but rest for a moment on a concern less obvious and significant as those listed above, specifically and namely the question of architecture.

That the event of 9/11 took place on the body and surface of architecture, or specifically the body and surface of two architectural edifices, namely the World Trade Center Twin Towers and the Pentagon, seems an obvious enough observation. That the fall-out and intellectual footprint of the event of 9/11 as a result of this observation might be able to be extended to architectural questions of a theoretical nature as a consequence of this fact is less so.

Given the event of 9/11 having played out upon the surface of architecture, and in the fact that significant pieces of architecture were destroyed by the attack, thought turned soon after to the redevelopment of the architectural edifices lost that day. In thought having turned toward thinking through a redevelopment of that which was destroyed, initial architectural questions toward redevelopment of Ground Zero in Lower Manhattan following the event of 9/11 were articulated most forthrightly by a number of architects and artists interviewed in the weeks immediately after the attack, providing a starting point for a mental blueprint for that which was desired to be seen (re)built on the site following the destruction of the Twin Towers, and hence articulate an architectural response.

In a September 30, 2001 *New York Times* article, Deborah Solomon surveyed a number of distinguished architects and artists as to what sort of response to redevelopment they might like to see on the site of Ground Zero. Amongst the varied voices that emerged from her interviews, a need for memorialization versus rebuilding was articulated, as one of two poles in which any redevelopment might take its course.[1] Amongst the rebuilding proponents (as opposed to memorialization) were a number of architects, such as Richard Meier, who voiced amongst other things, that, "We need office space, we need new buildings that are an even greater symbol of New York than what was there before".[2] Others echoed this sentiment, such as Robert A.M Stern, Dean of the School of Architecture Yale, who stated that, "We are still a brash, new, swaggering country, and we must still explore the imaginative possibilities of height. To bury our heads in the sand and create imaginary voids seems not appropriate."[3] From the vantage point of architects surveyed for this *New York Times* article, there was a desire, therefore, to see new buildings rise in the place of the Twin Towers from almost the moment they collapsed, and that any redevelopment proposal should be one of rebuilding. The die of redevelopment was eventually cast in favor of rebuilding on April 9 2002, with the Lower Manhattan Development Corporation (LMDC) unveiling a preliminary redevelopment vision for Lower Manhattan[4].

Such sentiments favoring and calling for rebuilding as documented by the *New York Times*, and the various desires surrounding it, were captured by Reinhold Martin in a highly insightful piece on the currency of the Twin Towers and the substance against which the event of 9/11 arguably unfolded, titled "One or More"[5]. In this article, Martin articulated a connection between the architecture of the Pentagon and that of the Twin Towers, situating the Twin Towers as an architectural extension of the sentiments (and we could also say desire, although not articulated by him through the specific use of this term) embodied by the Pentagon, thus situating the attack of 9/11 as an event that boiled down to one of attempting to destroy the networks of trade and global capital, which both the Pentagon and Twin Towers starkly embodied in their aspiration and architectural conception.

It is not necessary to reiterate the thrust of Martin's argument here, however illuminating it may be, on the meaning of the Twin Towers architecture and the architecture of that which was attacked, but it is perhaps necessary to offer his voice as a preliminary route to analyzing and evaluating the desire and sentiments of redevelopment captured by the reporting of the *New York Times*, which is to say the psychological genesis from which a redevelopment was to take form. Martin writes:

The political rhetoric and actions that have followed [the destruction of the Twin Towers] formulated around "good" versus "evil", "us" versus "them", and so on, have been largely directed toward restoring the security of this bubble, which is to say, to rebuilding it in both literal and a figurative sense [6].

The bubble that Martin alludes to is the networks of post-World War II trade and circulation embodied by the building of the Pentagon and that of the Twin Towers, and we might suggest the libidinal currency invested in them, in which he identifies the architecture of both the Pentagon and that of the Twin Towers to take shape[7] and against which the substance of the attack, he argues, was ultimately directed.

In examining such liminal gestures toward thinking through a possible redevelopment for Ground Zero, Martin alludes to a political rhetoric shaped around "us versus them", around "good versus evil", which took hold of both public, populist and political discourse following the event of 9/11, and found its way into the sentiments and desires for redevelopment, culminating in rebuilding. This is to say that the generation, creation and production of rebuilding, its genesis in other terms, lies within a subjectivity formulated by the sentiment of "good versus evil", and "us versus them", directing in turn the nature of that which was desired to be seen as edificial in the content of any rebuilding scheme. It is necessary to emphasize this fact, namely that the sentiments voiced by the US administration and the public at large alike, situated the attacks of 9/11 in a rubric of contestation between forces and flows of what they have termed simplistically as "darkness", and the "liberal" light of freedom that the US State and public alike believes to possess by virtue of their birthright. It is here argued, that it is precisely the content of this contestation of sentiment and desire that set the plane for the genesis (generation, creation, production) and subsequent proposals of redevelopment articulated for the site of Ground Zero following the attacks.

Through the lens of the *New York Times* article and Martin's analysis of redevelopment sentiments, we may rightly ask: what was the psychological genesis in which the redevelopment of Ground Zero became construed? Taking into consideration the statements of the two architects quoted above, which might be taken as representative of the sentiments favoring rebuilding, it was one of triumphalism over defeat, one of rebuilding and reconstruction over destruction, one of "good" triumphing "evil". The event-horizon on which we find the redevelopment of Ground Zero taking place is one articulated by "brashness" and "swagger", the desire to see something that is an "even greater symbol of New York than what was there before", a symbol and sign triumphing over the desire of the terrorists.

In the months that followed the clearing of Ground Zero from the rubble left behind by the destruction of the Twin Towers, and in the context of debate surrounding redevelopment versus memorialization, a citizens group of New York expressed this same sentiment and desire by hiring a billboard in SOHO, which read: "Rebuild the Towers, Bigger and Better than Before",[8] voicing a radical vision for the site in which the mistakes of the Twin Towers were destined to be blindly repeated again. This is stated as a means to point out that it was the Twin Towers' libidinal genesis itself that was being attempted to be transplanted and carried over into the creation, generation and production of any rebuilding, and thus the signification against which the attack on the Twin Towers was made was being desired arguably to be resurrected, with the potential that gave currency to the acts of that fateful day to be blindly repeated. This is stated not for wanting to evacuate the need for "big" or "better", but rather for wanting to highlight the substance of that "big" and "better" that is desired to be resurrected, namely a subjectivity and desire finding its way to architectural creation, generation and production that was beholden to the power represented in the capitalist circulation of which the Twin Towers was a sign, following Martin's previously referred to analysis.

The clamor to rebuild an edifice even bigger and better than before, and as a way to demonstrate the victory of "good" over "evil" demonstrated a populist thrust that lacked any analysis or comprehension of how the architectural accomplishment and architecture of the Twin Towers led to it being enveloped in an act of terrorism that contributed to and culminated in its ultimate destruction.

Conversely, the desire to see something "bigger and better" replace the Twin Towers, voiced by architects and society at large, failed to enter into any sober analysis of the forces of desire at play in the event. The play of forces in American society resultant to and let loose by the destruction of the Twin Towers seemed only to grasp a need for a re-expression of monumentalism and symbols of triumphalism over that or those who destroyed them. In this way, the libidinal currency of architects, government[9] and society at large voicing a triumphalist resurrection of the Twin Towers in a new development, construed a subjectivity whose genesis might only do justice to resurrecting the "iconomy"[10] of that which was destroyed as a reverberation of the Twin Towers' genesis in the redevelopment, an *a posteriori* articulation and construal of a sign-object as replacement, and the structure and architecture of that sign-object, of that which was destroyed.

This point is given further emphasis in the sequence of events surrounding redevelopment, whereby the initial Beyer Blinder Belle's presentation[11] of redevelopment schemes (be they master-plans only) at the Javits Center on July 20 2002, were hounded down by the press and public alike as not being imaginative or symbolic enough as architectural proposals. The public and press wanted to see something triumphalist and monumental replace the Twin Towers as opposed to banal, something in which the Twin Tower's "iconomy" was to be reflected, regardless of the substance of that "iconomy", and regardless of its inference upon the attack. It was this sentiment that was captured by the comments of *New York Times* architecture critic

Herbert Muschamp when he critiqued these initial LMDC proposals exhibited first at Federal Hall and then presented to the public at the Javits Center as an exercise in "breathtaking determination to think small"[12].

The lack (*manque*) that the destruction of the Twin Towers created in the subjective horizon of the socius of New York and broader American populace translated itself into a desire, whose genesis was expressed in varying ways for redevelopment by the LMDC final 7 designs for Ground Zero. The history and pattern of subjective construal and expression of desire that can be traced through the responses mustered by architects responding to interviews in the immediate aftermath of the attack, the public citizens' group expressing to recapture the substance of the Twin Towers, through to the popular and professional rejection of the initial LMDC proposals presented at the Javits Center, all share a common genesis in the lack of an "iconomy" power that the public sought in any redevelopment proposals, and an expression of a need to recapture it. Such a repeated subjective construal and expression of desire in relation to what might be seen as desirable to replace the Twin Towers might be suggested to lie in the absence of understanding of the iconomic structure of the Twin Towers and the subjective content that drove the attack on them.

In referring to the term "iconomy" it is, as Terry Smith points out[13], the "symbolic exchange" invested in and flowing from the architecture of that which was sought to replace the Twin Towers that is being defined. Such a "symbolic exchange" is reliant on an economy of representation and signification, a semiology by which the redeveloped scheme is imbued and with which it can be read. As can be gleaned from the above analysis, the representation and signification of redevelopment was desired to reflect and refract back, indeed recreate, the regime of symbolic exchange that the destroyed Twin Towers embodied. In doing so, the iconomic regime of the destroyed buildings was being sought by the socius in redevelopment – its "iconomy" by another term – was being sought to be regenerated, reproduced and recreated in the proposals for redevelopment.

In examining the relation between Terry Smith's term "iconomy" and that of libidinal economy, a libidinal economy is characterized by "systems", "energy" and "intensity", one that seeks a creation of meaning as residing in desiring-affects, which reside in and affect the individual and collective formation of subjectivity. Such an affect is always unleashed by an event, which unleashing causes new possibilities or creative movement to take place and, if coupled by a criticality in doing so, subverts the assignation of the sign[14].

If a mere replication of the representation, signification and semiology of the Twin Towers was being sought, the libidinal construct that could have arisen to critically subvert and resolve such assignation of the sign that was destroyed remains absent, leading to a blindly complicit construct coming into play that could be called myopic as opposed to learning from the act of the event. It is in this vein that Terry Smith asks: "...just want kind of regime of symbolic exchange, what kind of "iconomy", is coming into being?"[15] Instead of dissimulation as a force for new possibilities, critical and creative movement and the subversion of the sign as it existed in the destroyed Twin Towers, what we saw emerge was a desire for simulation of it in any redevelopment. It is in this way that we can assert that the complex inter-relationship between senses (subjectivity) and matter creating affect that is associated with libidinal eruption and the seeking of otherness was short-circuited in the professional, public and populist discourse and practice surrounding redevelopment. If the "iconomy" or the regime of symbolic exchange being sought for redevelopment had attempted to create a subversion of the symbolic economy of power as embodied in the Twin Towers and the Pentagon building, we might be able to say that a critical libidinal flow would have affected itself, and an entirely different approach to redevelopment would have been sought – an entirely different "iconomy" would have been pursued – and realized. Instead, the genesis, creation and production of "iconomy" being sought for redevelopment remained in a desire for erecting a sign that might regain and resurrect a symbol of *power* as dictated by the sentiment of lack originating from the destruction of the original buildings.

This analysis is made in a manner to not forsake or forget about the very practical need to provide a replacement for the lost leasable floor-space that was in the interest of Larry Silverstein, owner of the Twin Towers, in championing redevelopment. The question, however, becomes the way in which the various redevelopment proposals and the subsequently accepted and currently being realized schemes were conceived in their genesis, that is what generated, created and produced (gen) them to proceed in their substance of subjective imprint or subjectification of architectural possibilities (desire), in their very ideological foundations and genesis leading to a production and outcome. In as far as the ideological foundations and genesis of the design of redevelopment are concerned, it might be reiterated that the outcome and subjective source were to regain and resurrect a symbol of capitalist circulation and hence related State power as of the Twin Towers original, and thus could be said to be in collusion with the sentiments and subjectivity of capitalism and the content of the regime of the capitalist State as inherent in the original conception of the Twin Towers, and against which the liminal content the substance of the attack was arguably directed.

Raising then the question of architecture in relation to the libidinal band of the conception of the event, and construing the architecture of the Twin Towers as partaking in this libidinal band causing the event of 9/11 to take place as it did, it is necessary to begin to address the question of just what route redevelopment of any architecture on the site of Ground Zero might have taken given the subjective construal of architecture thus far raised, one that thinks through and apprehends the desire latent within redevelopment, and then critiques that desire for the purpose of articulating a different way to redevelopment, one that might resolve and comprehend the substance of the attacks.

As a response to a subjective construal of architecture in light of the above salient reading of 9/11 and the relation between architecture and the libidinal band, it is inadequate to suggest as a response to architectural consciousness that it merely requires a complex system of security features, surveillance and so-called counter-terrorism measures to be considered and adopted into future planning and design decisions, as some of the New York League of Architects' submissions suggested in the wake of 9/11[16].

Amongst the few worthwhile architectural evaluations of the attack of 9/11 in relation to architectural thought, Reinhold Martin's analysis stands out again as one more thoughtful. In his essay titled "Architecture at War – a report from Ground Zero", Martin posed the questions of "historical conditions" and the "historical (and political) dimensions"[17] that led to 9/11. Such a questioning and approach of thought provides an entry into analyzing the substance of 9/11 as an architectural event rooted in a milieu of political action fuelled by subjectivity. Even though Martin doesn't offer an analytical or theoretical response to this question in particular, the absence and silence that follows the posing of this question offers a thoughtful entry into an interrogation of the substance of 9/11. It is the silence following the posing of this question that begs for it an analysis that might view the event of 9/11 as something that goes far deeper than a random terrorist attack on ill-defined "freedoms" or a propaganda of "the free", and opens the possibility to articulate a response to it that resides in libidinal philosophy. It is from the root of this question that we can attempt to valorize the substance of the dual architectural-politico event of 9/11 as something that was libidinal and which resided in desire. We may reshape this question and ask not, "What led to 9/11?" but instead, "What was the substance of the architectural event of 9/11 and what responses might that substance muster?" The answer might suggest that it was a partial culmination of multiplicities leading to assemblages culminating in an event that unleashed libidinal forces in the act of those who carried it out. The more important question one might extrapolate from the silence following Martin's interrogation is: "What does the libidinal substance of the socio-architectural-politico event of 9/11 lend to rethinking architectural thought and how might that lead to a responsive[18] architectural redevelopment in its wake?"

Martin's response to this second question – preliminarily entered into by him in his essay through his analysis of the United Architects' proposal, and other projects, which formed the LMDC (Lower Manhattan Development Corporation) short-listed nine projects for the redevelopment of Ground Zero, is worth reiterating here. Martin dismisses the nature of architectural thought called on and championed by *New York Times* architecture critic Herbert Muschamp – and responded to by United Architects and others either consciously or not – as an exercise in "aesthetics as politics"[19], namely that "by enthusiastically accepting such protocols "progressive" architects showed themselves unprepared and perhaps unwilling to unbind the chains that link their production to the cultural logic of regressive power"[20]. Martin makes this analytical claim in light of United Architects' use of military-capitalist-politico terminology accompanying the rationalization of United Architects design proposal, such as "performance", "instrumentality" and Greg Lynn's own term of, "to collapse the boundary between global military conflict and everyday life" as a theoretical justification for their scheme[21]. Such terminology of justification positions the architectural and ideological response to 9/11 as exhibited in the LMDC final 7 schemes in general, and in United Architects' proposal in particular, as a "gesture made *in the service of* an emboldened sense of empire and war on all fronts, and not against it."[22] Such an assessment is quite damning on the architectural thought represented by the élan of architecture practice chosen for the LMDC final 7.

What the analysis of the approach and thought of United Architects' proposal's evaluation – and other proposals – testifies to, is that architects themselves, like society at large, became caught up in the assemblage of desire voiced by the US adminis-tration, many commentators and the public alike following the attack of 9/11. A libidinal event never dissipates into entropy, but rather conversely, sets off at right angles into further reverbera-tions and libidinal production – it redoubles itself and spreads through the multi-directional polymorphous body of the socius to create politics. This is the substance of the libidinal event as politics, the substance of politics as such, of how politics is propagated by an event, and architects – as it seems from Martin's analysis – were not immune to partaking and giving voice to the reverberated assemblages set off by the event of the attack presented to us, and embraced by society at large.

Conversely to the elevation of micro-fascisms onto a global political and consequential architecture arena, what is required is not a retreat into defensive and retaliatory politics of form in collusion with the State, as United Architects' proposal might suggest in light of Martin's analysis of it, but rather an open rethinking of the implications of the libidinal economy on thought and action, in particular architectural thought and consequential action (taking possession of place / coming into form / coming into appearance), especially in light of a libidinal event's such spectacular co-option of architecture as what 9/11 was. What is important and necessary, is to examine the possible micro-flows of movement within thought and desire as emanating from 9/11, and deconstruct the way to a possible thought and consequential action (politics) that makes sense of it – and of us, of our beliefs and of our desires – and the essence of architecture – in light of the attacks.

Following Deleuze, a flow or micro-flow and any micro-politics that may result from it, is "always of belief and of desire"[23]. What we (in America or the West more generally) collectively encountered as a result of 9/11 was an attack and then apprehension of our belief and desire vested in our society as represented to us by the State and its values; our micro-flow of value, that by which we are signified and represented, and by which the world – our world – is reflected back to us, that is Us – was confronted. This confrontation of a micro-flow sets off a libidinal micro-politics of desire at what might be considered a molecular organization. For the collective "us", 9/11 brought into question the structure and foundation of our micro-politics – and shattered it; (as iterated above, 9/11 should be viewed as a war on subjectivity, rather than a war on terror). In the least, 9/11 should have caused the collective Us to sit up and take stock of ourselves as we are vested in our belief and in our desire – and in turn the substance and essence of that vested in architecture and in our taking place. It should have unleashed a requisite reorientation of our belief and desire in an omnipotent macro-politics as repre-sented to us by the State and its institutions, and began a questioning of just how we begin to take possession of space and create a placing for the site of Ground Zero given the nature and substance of the event of 9/11.

The State, of course, took another tack and represented the event of 9/11 to us as the first salvo of war. It is in this light, that we can appreciate Martin's analysis of United Architects' proposal as being "unwilling to unbind the chains that link their production to the cultural logic of regressive power" (in the same manner as how many architects are unable and unwilling to unbind the chains of market consumerism and from their architecture).

In as far as United Architects' proposal failed to deal with the re-evaluation and deconstruction of the foundation and structure of our collective micro-politics, that is our collective (Western) belief and desires, and everything that flows from it – including into architecture – and at which we find the basis of all architectural thought and action, it must be relegated to the scrapheap of thought. Instead, as Martin rightly points out, United Architects – despite encompassing some of the most distinguished individuals to emerge on the architecture scene in the past decade and a half – re-articulated in its scheme the response that the State took to 9/11, and what the State might have desired to be seen by and in any architectural response to its stance and the event; United Architects' politics and consequential action fell in line and became a quasi spokesperson for the macro, rather than deconstructors of the micro, as what any creative intellectual response ought to have been. Martin eludes to the necessity of deconstruction following the architectural event of 9/11 through his terminology of "historical and political dimensions", even if he doesn't call it the beginnings of deconstruction of the event of 9/11 by name. The event of 9/11 as it bears on architecture requires just such a deconstructive process of micro-politics, that is of our and the Western world's libidinal economy – desire and belief – that the LMDC final 7 and subsequently commissioned and now being realized schemes failed to take. It is in this deconstructive approach taken to the desire and belief that forms our libidinal economy – that is thought, desire and feeling – that any possible architecture can be brought forth anew as a result of 9/11 through us for redevelopment of Ground Zero and for further fields of action also, and in general.

What is meant by a call to such deconstruction following the event of 9/11 on architecture? The only thing that can be proffered is what Lyotard terms as *"durcharbeitung"* or "reworking" as articulated in his essay "Rewriting Modernity"[24], which is not a remembering (as in the structuralist cases for redevelopment put forth by the Meier/Eisenman/Seigal/Holl proposal or that of the Think group proposal and others), but rather a *working through* of thought in relation to architecture and in relation to the libidinal (desire) – the two together and in a reciprocal linked relation to one another: to raise architecture as a possibility of thought in the context of the event of 9/11 for the purposes of a critical architectural praxis resulting in redevelopment.

The term "reworking" is taken by Lyotard from Freud's use of the term *"durcharbeitung"*, meaning:

> ...a working attached to a thought of what is constitutively hidden from us in the event and the meaning of the event, hidden not merely by past prejudice, but also by those dimensions of the future marked by the pro-ject, the pro-grammed, pro-spectives, and even by the pro-position and the pro-posal to psychoanalyze[25].

That is, architectural thinking should have placed itself on the couch and engaged that which it had learnt earlier from certain circles[26], rekindling a pro[27]-active priority or stance in relation to thought. It is through such *"durcharbeitung"* that we clearly reveal the failings of the LMDC final 7 and subsequently commissioned and currently being realized schemes, which constituted not so much a working through of the event of 9/11, but rather an exercise in the production of signs that may do justice perhaps to the response of the State and Power, but not to thought. Conversely, reworking or working through the event of 9/11 in relation to architecture, aims to return architecture to the analyst's couch once more and find the associative condition between sets of substrates, and link or thread them together in a way that they open up interpretation on an event, rather than close it down – it is the opposite of a structuralist narrative, and perhaps the opposite of what the State might desire to see and support from within its striated structure, but nonetheless necessary as an initial theoretical articulation and response to an event such as 9/11 and its implications on architecture and more importantly subjectivity – the two of which are inseparable from one another and inalienable in their individual consideration.

In raising the question of a necessary *durcharbeitung*, that is a working through of an approach to redevelopment, and in raising it for the purposes of offering a different and other way to architecture in light of the libidinal (desire-based) valorization and understanding of 9/11 and in the context of construing architecture as an immanent condition that operates from the inside-out, it is necessary to ask just what it is actually that needs to be examined and addressed in order for this reworking to occur. In other words, how should have any necessary working through of architecture for the site of Ground Zero commenced, and what might it have needed to examine?

The only address one can make to this question, which is a question of the subjective construal of any rebuilding effort, is one that learns from the libidinal cause of the event of 9/11 and the destruction of the Twin Towers, and alternatively learns from and counters the reverberations that surfaced in response to it in the American socius, that is one that seeks to disrupt striated figuration from any architecture that might proceed on the site of Ground Zero; such a learning and comprehension is the genesis by which any *durcharbeitung* might proceed on that site. Such disruption is sought as a displacement of power and its affect in the representation of the politics of the State and capitalism, and is meant as a readdress to the cause and architecture of the event of 9/11 in the face of the destruction of the Twin Towers. It is in this desire that a disruption and dislodgement of power with force might be actualized – that is to say a disruption of *puovoir* (power) in favor of *puissance* (force).

The desire for *puissance* (force) over *pouvoir* (power) is as a means to create affects and figuration of heterogeneity and otherness by way of, in and through architecture, as opposed to striated affects. The only address to architecture in the face of the event of 9/11 is to seek and desire an otherness from power through architecture, and an otherness for the subject inhabiting that architecture, an otherness that seeks to disrupt the affects of this power on the person's subjectivity in inhabiting and using that space in particular. This otherness and heterogeneity must be sought from the very genesis of redevelopment, its subjective construal of generation, production and creation; such a struggle, is what Foucault has termed as a "struggle for a new subjectivity"[28]. It is through struggling for a new subjectivity in architecture, specifically for any architecture that might be created on the site of Ground Zero, that a *durcharbeitung* of architecture might be realized, and it is in the accomplishment of this struggle and the thought that goes into constructing it, that architecture can answer its call to be raised as a possibility for thought.

In addressing the phenomena and representation of power (*pouvoir*) in architecture, it is the space and function of the sign that is being apprehended, for as Lyotard writes in *Libidinal Economy*, "There is no sign or thought of the sign which is not about power and for power."[29] One can therefore not talk about power and the thought of power in architecture without talking about the space, function, figuration and representation of the sign. It is only in disrupting the space and function of the sign, that a heterogeneity can come about in architecture. This is a question of "iconomy", of just what sort of "iconomy" is intended to be represented in that which is redeveloped. The antagonism of signs and their relation to architecture is the precise problematic that is found in both the destruction of the Twin Towers and the problems with the proposals for redevelopment. This antagonism is one that is caught up with the State's reproduction of itself and its libidinal economy in and through architecture, and specifically in the official proposals of the various redevelopment schemes. The challenge therefore to this libidinal eruption is a challenge that must be had with power, and as such with the sign. It is only in challenging and then disrupting the relationship between the sign and power that architecture would have been able to begin to enter into any meaningful redevelopment of Ground Zero following the event of 9/11. Furthermore, if power (*pouvoir*) and force (*puissance*) are oppositional concepts to one another, as indeed Lyotard uses them in *Libidinal Economy*, then the affects and figural representation of force are the oppositional representation to the figural act of the sign.

Following this quote concerning the sign and power, Lyotard goes on to discuss and critique the nature of the sign and semiotics, finishing by saying, "Don't even hope to catch the libidinal in these nets"[30], which is to say, that the representation of libidinal desire that might be befitting to any architectural production at Ground Zero, an architectural production that disrupts the representation of the politics of the State as capitalism, cannot be brought forth by an "iconomy" that depends on a construal of the sign. The only way a libidinal construal of any efficacy could have been brought about at Ground Zero, and by doing so avert the event of 9/11 from repeating itself, is by architecture producing a creation and production that is devoid of the sign, that is to say devoid of a representation of power, instead valorizing the figuration of libidinal intensities of a nature that are in opposition to those of the figural representation of striated power. In its stead, it is an architectural production of force that would have been required, akin to some of the strategies developed by the Situationists, or developed at least in the same spirit of critique of representation as what they forwarded. One cannot catch an efficacious libidinal outcome for Ground Zero in the nets of power, nor, it must be said, can one awaken a required readdress of the libidinal through power and its representations of striation to which the sign lends itself.

"Thus the sign is enmeshed in nihilism, nihilism proceeds by signs; to continue to remain in semiotic thought is to languish in religious melancholy and to subordinate every intense emotion to a lack and every force to finitude."[31] This passage from Lyotard, read together with the previous passages quoted earlier, suggests that the figural representations of power, which the sign by nature always refers to and creates, is always enmeshed in nihilism, that it subordinates every intense emotion to lack, and every force to finitude, that it counters and extinguishes the production of force, that it creates the opposite affects to that of the representations of force. Conversely this is to say that the only way intense emotion, desire and force are able to be presented in and through the figural is through a representation that dissimulates and disrupts power and the striated.

What is required in light of the State's co-option of architecture into its libidinal band following the event of 9/11 and present in the proposals for redevelopment, is not a search for and erection of striated signs in the vein of networked spaces of trade, but rather a challenge to the logic of production of signs in architecture all together, or a way in which they might be rearticulated. The only way that the "iconomy" of anything that is built on Ground Zero can escape, or at least disrupt the space and representation of the politics and space of the State as capitalism and its libidinal structure, the only strategy that would have held out any libidinal efficacy for redevelopment, is the entering into an architectural production of dissimulation. Lyotard defines dissimulation as "difference within identity, the chance event within the foresight of composition, passion within reason – between each, so absolutely foreign to each other, the strictest unity..."[32] that is a movement toward the disruption of striated characteristics of architecture toward the smooth, through which a dissimulation occurs, realizing the representation of the process of this disruption.

Lyotard talks about dance to illustrate dissimulation, saying that such a dance would then be "...not composed and notated, but on the contrary, one in which the body's gesture would be, with the music, its timbre, its pitch, intensity and duration, and with the words (dancers are also singers), at each point in a unique relation, becoming at every moment an emotional event..."[33] A dance therefore that disrupts striated representation and the semiotic hierarchy between music and body, and conversely fuses the two into a new ensemble, one that sets each other in motion, one in which the distinction of power of one upon the other is suspended: pure force. The analogy of such dance in relation to an architectural dissimulation, would mean as Deleuze has written about characteristics of smooth space, "Continuous variation, continuous development of form;... [and] the pure act of the drawing of a diagonal across the vertical and horizontal."[34] – that is characteristics that are not dissimilar to some of the figural representation harnessed in some instances by a few in the contemporary digital architecture avant-garde, and noted about Kas Oosterhuis and Ilona Lénárd's (Oosterhuis.nl) proposal for redevelopment. Any body of architecture intended for Ground Zero should have harnessed and entered the realm and figural representation of such pure force[35].

If architecture at Ground Zero could have set out on this route toward a production through a different genesis to that which was entered upon, then the power of the sign might have had the potential to be disrupted, and an architecture of dissimulation forwarded. The resultant "iconomy" of any such creation would have dissipated into and be as Lyotard writes, "productive of movement"[36], beget subjective construal, a "construction of other things, texts, images, sounds, politics, caresses..."[37] etc, creating a "different reaction, a different reception"[38], in other words a heterogeneity and otherness, an opening onto smooth characteristics of occupation, an architecture that attempts to liberate the users from power and the affects of power and striation, in order to arrive at a truly deconstructed response to the event of 9/11, a deconstructive response entered into and addressed in, by and through architecture.

When using the term heterogeneous desire in relation to the libidinal economy throughout this essay, its semantics are denoted by the splayed-out sexual body and its ephemeral skin with which Lyotard commences *Libidinal Economy*[39] – a very much real and living experiential effect and all-consuming feeling, one that is exactly the same as that which we have all experienced in our lust toward another person's body and sex. Desire is real, it is penetrating, wanting to be penetrated, and all consuming, it controls one's thoughts and emotions begetting a need for gratification and resolution; it is in this same sense that the term "desire" needs to be understood as used and denoted by the term "libidinal economy" in the present writing. It is a real experiential state of body and mind creating heterogeneous flow and dissimulated habitation of place and occupation.

All this having been said, the words of Deleuze and Guattari echo through our thought: "Never believe that a smooth space will suffice to save us"[40]. Smooth space in itself, as iterated above, can never exist outside a certain move toward and envelopment by striation, just as when architecture is proposed for redevelopment, an immediate striation is entered upon in taking possession of place. However, it must also be prudent to be reminded of Chtcheglov's words, that:

> Architecture is the simplest means of articulating time and space, of modulating reality, of engendering dreams. It is a matter not only of plastic articulation and modulation expressing an ephemeral beauty, but of a modulation producing influences in accordance with the eternal spectrum of human desires and the progress of realizing them.[41]

In having begun to circumscribe an argument for the nature and type of redevelopment of Ground Zero, how might such propositions result in an actual proposal for redevelopment and building? Taking the Situationist practice-concepts of *dérive* and *detournement* as starting points to begin to guide ways of actual development, the following questions need to be kept in mind:

- How does one begin to create an experience of a different or heterogeneous occupation of space and the urban environment?
- How does one begin to create new thoughts and new feelings in users of a space in the face of regular, mundane, repetitive behavior, behavior of the everyday that are governed by striation, such as work tasks and the daily routine of work?
- How does one begin to activate the sedentary with affects, intensities and events, to allow *haecceities* to infiltrate the subjective construal and conception of making place, occupying space and taking place. To make architecture a real taking of place, that is an orchestration that sets off events other than those embodied by the Twin Towers?

To answer these pertinent questions, a possible fortuitous proposal for redevelopment would not have been the design of a building *per se*, but rather a written articulation of ways to *proceed* with building that could be called a directive for redevelopment or a guide, a set of loose regulations that has as its aim to bring forth the characteristics and experiences of new thoughts, new feelings, intensities and *haecceities* as spelled out above, and aim to minimize the regulation of function and form. Such a set of regulations, as it were in a contradictory manner of minimizing regulation, could have achieved two things: first they would have acted as a bind as to what shouldn't happen on the site, whilst at the same time acting as an opportunity for realizing collective invention.

What such a framework or directive might suggest, is a

redevelopment effort that takes on no hierarchy of space and function, but rather begins to meld all the various functions and uses of the intended occupiers of the space into a single "hotch-potch" or beehive-like space. In achieving such extreme mix-use the collective outcome of redevelopment might envisage retail, residential, commercial office space, indeed even light-industrial, educational and religious spaces and any and all other possible function to be realized in the one ensemble for the purposes of creating heterogeneity, not only in the character of spaces to be built, but also in the constitution of its users. I would imagine exceedingly numerous exit and entry points into the structure(s), with a cacophony of lift-wells – some or most external – staircases and other paths of egress cris-crossing the entire site.

In setting this out, a regulatory framework for redevelopment, not a building design, is required; one which allows individuals, companies and organizations to develop the site and build on it as they see fit, with respective spaces of development being "jumbled" on top and next to one another without any manner of hierarchy.

What such directive would suggest, is a creation of multiple modes of movement through the site in the vein of Constant's "New Babylon" project, most public – movement, arrival and departure that cris-crosses all the various functions and space of users. The aim of this development directive would be to create an ensemble where multiplicity of use and function come to co-inhabit each other and together begin to create form. Not to assign form, but to allow the users to create form in a free-flow manner as they each might want to use their respective space and the ensemble of spaces together, creating a "mish-mash" of an ensemble that is essentially formless in the true sense of the word across the entire site. The height of it might not be limited, merely each new development's structural codification and resultant form of architecture would need to obviously adhere to not collapsing.

The only thing that I can think of as the closest form that this might result in is akin to Hundertwasser's Haus in Vienna, and other architecture of Hundertwasser's, but even more chaotically ordered and built: like a beehive gone wrong (built by bees high on dope as some entomologist might suggest) crossed with the form of a Rio De Janeiro slum proceeding up the hillside, or akin to some of the village elevations in the Cinque Terre region of Liguria in Italy. Indeed it is not the form of the resultant structure(s) that is important, but rather the *experience* of users and the *mode* of use in and across the site: the form that this might result in is of not much importance. By initiating development in such a manner, the resultant architecture might "…at least initially, be a means of experimenting with a thousand ways of modifying life, with a view to a mythic synthesis."[42]

What such directive would imagine is a development that creates a microcosm of a city in a way that the development would invite a "re-imagination as an oneiric realm open to exploration and discovery, an ocean with its own depths and expanse."[43] By doing so, the various tactics of the Situationists would come into play, resulting in a development that is "unconfined by the rationalism [striation] and function of the State, and which are instead formed along lines of emotion, irrationality, and accident"[44], or in other words create "continuous variation, continuous development of form;… [and] the pure act of the drawing of a diagonal across the vertical and horizontal"[45], or "constant modulation in accord with the continually changing aspects of our existence such as we will produce it."[46]

The purpose of such a deregulated "regulation" would be to:

…counter the bounded, privatized building or urban square of mono-functional intentions with variable spaces and atmosphere, spaces with no particular boundaries (whether physical or mental), with spaces of change and indeterminacy. Above all, these are spaces of the unexpected, unexpected forms, unexpected events, unexpected collisions and sounds, unexpected anythings.[47]

For example, one might be able to hear hammering on metal and the sound of welding, or indeed the sound of children and religious services through openings onto a Forex trading floor adjacent to a convenience store entrance.

Such a tactic would therefore create "dynamic environments related to styles of behavior", that is create affect that will displace the everyday modes of ingrained behavior to do with a mono-cultural office environment, space and perception toward an ensemble that offers the opportunity to the user of the space to recognize and engage representation that disrupts and critiques it.

Such a non-hierarchical, beehive-like structure would act only as a starting point for modulating behavior in and across the site and its users, inviting non-expected junctions in experience and behavior, affecting perceptions, thoughts and feelings about ownership, movement and work – and life in general – but also create the beginnings or at least potential for deterritorializing toward smooth habitation, and begin to function as a direct critique of the striated networked space of trade as vested in the image of Capitalism and the State. It is in such a way that a taking possession of place and the creation of space might delimit the striated and open-up toward the accidental, begetting the smooth. It is in such a way that we might identify multiple single threads "wherein architecture (as encounter) emerges as the locus of a new subjectivity"[48]. This having been said, it remains only as a provisional idea toward redevelopment, the final outcome of which would be indeterminable and constantly changing.

John Cage's *Improvisations 1B* is a good example of such dereg-ulated structure and sequence, albeit in music. The sound of *Improvisations 1B* is produced by way of a non-structured yet symphonic plucking on cacti and other various non-ordered rattles of flora, whereby certain elements of possible sound are given, but producing a non-hierarchical ensemble, just as certain elements of construction technology and type might be given, but could be used in a non-hierarchical chance way as to create an improvised oneiric sound-scape. In the case of construction elements vis-à-vis building construction and resultant architecture, the result becomes a chance unification of elements jumbled together as they might arise for purposes of use, behavior therein, function and/or form. What results aesthetically from this cacophony is not important, but rather how the space is experienced and used as a result, which in turn ultimately finds an echo in its iconomic signification or alternatively in its very dissimulation of signification. It is in this play of resultant use, form and behavior that any pre-determined hierarchy can be broken down, and the space given over to chance encounters, rhythms of play and discovery along the contours of the Situationist's practices of *dérive*, returning the site of Ground Zero and what ensues on it to uses, behaviors, form and function that imbue the complex of its spaces with heterogeneity and the resultant breaking down of capitalist semiology, and through it creating the promise of the formulation of new subjectivities.

The Possibility for Architecture Theory

The concern of this essay is to schematically outline and place into context the approach to thinking through issues architectural that might valorize a turn toward theory in the discipline of architecture. By doing so, my intention is to briefly outline and justify a process by which a possibility for architecture theory might follow. My intention is to open up a way toward understanding architecture, and in consequence to place it in a different light, a light from which a certain practice, process and application might follow.

By way of unfolding the term "thinking through issues architectural", I connect its understanding to a derivation of the etymology of the term "think", which according to the *Oxford Concise Dictionary of English Etymology*, denotes the action of "caus[ing] to appear to oneself"[1]. To think and to think through something therefore denotes a condition of "coming forth into appearance", a process and state intrinsically connected to vision and sight on the one hand, and to presence on the other; one could say it is to behold a visual presence of something in one's thought. As such, the act of "thinking through something" is primarily concerned with a schema of mental conception; the route toward this mental conception of presence is arrived at through contemplation and speculation, hence looking at a thing. This later etymology is precisely that which defines the Greek term *"theōrós"*[2], meaning "spectator", specifically referring to a vision on the other. To think through something and arrive at a presence of thought that can be visualized and then uttered, or written down, thus requires acting as a thoughtful spectator. It is this relation of a thoughtful spectator upon the discipline and process of architectural production that is the philosophical prerequisite in arriving at a possibility for architecture theory.

The reason it is "theory" that is being polemically traced, as opposed to "criticism", is that as K. Michael Hays writes in his Introduction to *Architecture Theory Since 1968*, architectural discourse since the 1960s has been concerned primarily with the construction of theory in relation to discussing issues architectural, as opposed to "criticism" – which would mean a certain definitive judgment on architecture – which it has displaced[3]. It is important to ask why theory has come to supersede criticism since the 1960s, and consequently why K. Michael Hays asserts his statement?

Terry Eagleton quotes Elizabeth Bruss in his book *The Function of Criticism*, that theory "arises whenever the function of criticism is itself in doubt"[4]. Eagleton goes on to write that: "Theory... does not emerge at just any historical moment; it comes into being when it is both possible and necessary, when the traditional rationales for a social or intellectual practice have broken down and new forms of legitimization for it are needed."[5]

The social context for theory's emergence in liberal humanism can be dated back to the decade of the 1960s, when universities greatly expanded their student numbers, causing a previously unseen mix of class, gender, race and ethnicity to take presence within their walls, which sociality came to question the dominant forms of liberal humanism hitherto practiced in academia, namely criticism. It was as a result of a questioning of the dominant forms of thinking in academia that the genre of theory emerged and by which criticism was challenged. The rise of an antagonistic genre of thinking and writing, which asks less so the question, "What is going on?" as opposed to the more impatient question, "What the hell is all this?"[6] did not leave architecture discourse untouched – it is in the voicing of, "What the hell is all this?" that the thoughtful spectator reaches her utterance. In turn it is in the frame of such utterance that a theoretically infused architectural discourse emergent since the 1960s found its place, distinctly within the mould of an attempt

to "think architecture and its possibilities through" as a speculation, as opposed to arriving at a judgment. Such an approach is
necessary precisely because the framework of architectural
discourse associated with architecture theory, as the 1960s have
shown, is something that only a cantankerous troubling can do
justice to. This being said, however, a judgment in consequence
of certain theorizing might necessarily be always present, but
only insofar as it is derived from the act of theorization.

K. Michael Hays presents an erudite articulation of the role
and practice of theory in architecture since the 1960s in his
Introduction in *Architecture Theory Since 1968*. Hays writes that,
"...architecture theory is a practice of mediation. In its strongest
form mediation is the production of relationships between formal
analyses of a work of architecture and its social ground or
context..."[7] This mediation between formal analyses of actual
works of architecture and a social ground or context is produced,
as Hays referring to Fredric Jameson says, by:

> ...the setting into active equivalence of two pre-existing codes,
> which thereby, in a kind of molecular ion exchange, become a
> new one. What must be understood is that the new code (or
> meta-code) can in no way be considered a synthesis of the
> pair... it is rather a question of linking two sets of terms in
> such a way that each can express and indeed interpret the
> other.[8]

It is through such linking and "setting into active equivalence of
two pre-existing codes" that one can argue for the privileging of
theory in a disciplinary process, be it architectural or otherwise.
This process is none other than applying a philosophically
oriented theoretical speculation to the process of thinking
something through. As Hays writes further in his Introduction,
this "mediatory function releases unnoticed complicities and
commonalities between different realities that were thought to

remain singular, divergent, and differently constituted."[9]

In departing from this initial excursus on the role of theory, it is necessary to place into context the contemporary practice in architecture discourse emergent from the 1960s onwards with previous pursuits of architectural theory historically. In Peter Eisenman's 1963 PhD thesis titled *The Formal Basis of Modern Architecture*, the thesis is concluded by outlining two types of theory that have governed architectural discourse since the Renaissance as inherited from the ancient architectural treatise author Vitruvius. The two types of theory Eisenman outlines are what he terms as "closed-ended" theory on the one hand, and "open-ended" theory on the other. Eisenman analyses the nature of theory and writing on architecture resultant from Vitruvius' *Ten Thesis on Architecture* beginning with Renaissance treatise author Alberti's *On the Art of Building in Ten Thesis*, through to Durand and later eighteenth and nineteenth century architectural treatise authors such as Guadet and Choisy. Eisenman identifies these texts as belonging to a classical Vitruvian-Albertian tradition, in as far as they treat the subject matter of architecture in a self-referential manner, in a way that the treatises' subject and object are both architecture. Such theorization Eisenman labels as "closed-ended", theorization that views and discusses architecture as being unchanging and unchangeable, always referring back to itself as an end. In opposition to this lineage and type of architectural theory, Eisenman posits and argues for the polemical essay as a type and genre of architectural theory that has the ability to transform architectural discourse from the "closed-ended" schema of the Vitruvian-Albertian kind, toward one that treats the subject matter of architecture in a manner that "allows for expansion and continuous application"[10], or in other words "open-ended". It is this type of discourse and architectural writing that Eisenman labels as the basis for the polemical essay in architecture.

Following Eisenman's analysis of these two types of differing approaches to the modes of architectural discourse, speculative and "open-ended" on the one hand and judgmental and "closed-ended" on the other, it is the model of the speculative polemical essay as theory that is presently being argued for as a means to process, and doing so for the purpose of evacuating the construction, or even analysis, of a set of "closed-ended" rules and prescriptions, and instead aiming to synthesize disparate texts and utilize their content for the aim of understanding something about the context of architecture in its ever-changing condition. Eisenman writes in this regard, that "to this end, theory should not be considered as a set piece, a neatly wrapped package, but rather as a continuously applicable and open-ended methodology"[11], or in other words "a possible way of approach to an architectural problem"[12], a process that thinks through issues architectural from disparate grounds.

Further to Eisenman's "open-ended" theoretical genre of architectural thinking, one must argue for an approach of "inter-disciplinarity", in the vein that Jane Rendell argues for it in her introduction to *Critical Architecture* (2007). In this introduction Rendell writes that it is possible for various "disciplinary approaches brought together – or which have yet to be brought together – within architecture to exert critical pressure on one another; I would describe the moments, projects and practices where this occurs as inter-disciplinary"[13]. Rendell further iterates in this same introduction, that the aim of bringing critical pressure to bear on disciplines is "to critique the modes of operation of those disciplines"[14]. The purpose therefore of pursuing an inter-disciplinary approach in architecture theory is to produce an "open-ended" and polemical critique. The purpose of this "open-ended" polemical writing is to harness an excursion into such inter-disciplinarity toward the thinking through of possibilities for the discipline of architecture, producing an insight, or at least a considered argument, on the new in turn.

Such an approach is one of attempting to create "political critique"[15], as much as it is of attempting to create an architectural critique *by way of theory*. Indeed, the critique of the political and a critique of the architectural in the process of pursuing architecture theory go hand-in-hand without any possibility of separation between the two. This is to say that when one thinks by way of theory, by default, one is thinking politically, in and through multiplicitous substrates of knowledge that have accumulated and come to bear on the possibility of a disciplinary practice. It is such thinking through of both the political and the architectural, and indeed in its course through the social, philosophical, psychiatric, psychoanalytical[16] and even psycho-sociological, that inter-disciplinarity reveals itself not as an affectation, but as a necessary and requisite route through which theory and subsequent critique based on that theory can unfold. As Rendell states: "The aim of such work is to question dominant processes that seek to control intellectual and creative production, and instead generate new resistant forms and modes of knowledge and understanding"[17].

In addressing the writing of critical architecture theory within the genre of critical theory, K. Michael Hays asserts "that for him the term "critical" [is] derived from critical theory and could be summed up as "the constant imagination, search for, and constructions of alternatives"."[18] It is in this vein, that any theorization of the architectural, perhaps seemingly at times subjective and speculative in nature, but nonetheless rigorous in its search for an interpenetration of philosophy with architectural thinking proceeds, an interpenetration that aims to "search for constructions of alternatives", and open up an understanding of both architecture and society in turn, indeed vis-à-vis each other.

This seemingly subjective and speculative manner of the interpenetrative use of philosophy with questions of architecture is done for the purposes of attempting to rethink and rework architectural thought and subsequent action, to think through and to show, in a manner, how an architectural process might be, or could potentially be constructed, or constructed otherwise. In so far as this is achieved, the reworking enabled by a philosophically oriented architectural enquiry acts as a route toward a critical theory of architectural discourse, and a critical route toward architectural practice. In this manner the method of a philosophically oriented architectural enquiry, similarly to a method of deconstruction in philosophy, aims not to demolish architectural discourse in a negative sense, but rather to circumscribe it in a positive sense. This positive circumscription of architectural discourse enabled by way of an interpenetrative use of philosophy on concerns architectural attempts to show how architecture discourse might be constructed anew, and the process of architectural practice thought afresh.

Vincent Descombes writes of philosophical Deconstruction, that its aim was to "show how philosophical discourses are constructed"[19]. In terms of borrowing from and applying the same methodology to architecture theory, deconstruction in architecture theory would be to show how "architectural discourses are constructed", and in view of that, how they could be constructed anew for the purposes of creative practice. In contradistinction, however, to Deconstruction in philosophical discourse, whereby Deconstruction "attempts to propose a "theory of philosophical discourse""[20], deconstruction in critical architecture theory attempts to find a new route to architectural truths and understandings for the purpose of architectural production. Just as Andrew Benjamin has stated in his *Architectural Philosophy:*

>...architectural theory has to be interconnected – perhaps even inter-articulated – with the actual activity of architecture... the argument has to be that it is the... thinking in which the activity of philosophy and theory combine, that marks out the

space for another formulation of architectural theory[21].

It is this combination of philosophy with theory for the purpose of another formulation of architecture that denotes the method and action of deconstruction in architecture. It is this that is at the heart of the methodology of all polemical, even creative thinking. For this purpose, and hence as a logical consequential necessity, architecture theory embraces a philosophical disposition for the purposes of understanding something about architecture in relation to its contexts, and then extending and extrapolating the implications of this understanding to a way of thinking about architecture in practice, and in consequence to its myriad contexts, whilst at the same time and in conclusion, always keeping an eye out for the practicalities of an actual utilization of its implications for architectural production. Rendell writes quoting Derrida: "that we give up the frontier and cease drawing lines to separate design [production] and criticism[22] [theory], that we look instead to sites of contamination – perhaps of inter-disciplinarity – for these call into question existing definitions and demand instead new forms of critical and creative work"[23] – both in the genre of critical architecture theory, and ultimately in the practice of architecture as well. In other words, and necessarily so, the explicit purpose of the philosophically oriented architectural enquiry is to shed light on possible action (and critical action at that) following a particular philosophical understanding; it is one of keeping an eye on both theory and practice, on how theory might first evaluate and theorize practice and then contaminate it to produce critical architecture in turn. As Rendell writes: "In a world that currently remains in the grips of an unjust corporate and imperialistic capitalism, critical architecture is urgently required."[24]

The pre-occupation of a theoretical discussion of a way to knowledge must always be coupled with a theoretical way of understanding society and culture, the two of which (knowledge on the one hand, and society and culture on the other) cannot be discussed independently of each other – it is this that provides architecture's critical context. This coupling of knowledge >< society/culture needs to be discussed with a view toward its concern with architectural thinking and conception, and ultimately action. It is by way of such process that architectural thinking is aimed to be rethought and reworked; in as far as the thinking contained in the theory succeeds in this, the process becomes a work of architectural deconstruction. As Ben Agger writes in his article "Critical Theory, Post-structuralism, Post-modernism: Their Sociological Relevance", "Critical theory by necessity generates deconstructive readings of cultural works and practices"[25], and it is to this purpose that an inter-disciplinary method of critical enquiry must be put to use. Given the nature of the philosophically oriented enquiry that the methodology of architecture theory must arguably follow, its intellectual lineage rooted in speculation marks it as an "open-ended" inter-disciplinary polemical enquiry in the vein of how Eisenman espouses it.

As eighteenth century French architect Boullée has stated: "The production of the mind is what constitutes architecture"[26]; the way in which the context of architecture theory is presently being outlined is what lends itself to the particular constitution of such production. Furthermore and in relation to this statement of Boullée's, it is pertinent to quote Guattari as an enabling rationale and context for the possibility of the polemical "open-ended" theory: "There are two methods of receiving theoretical statements: the academic's way is to take, or leave, the text as it stands, whereas the enthusiast's way is to take it and leave it, manipulating it as he sees fit, trying to use it to throw light on his circumstances and direct his life."[27] In a systematic and directed reading of texts for the purpose of shedding light on a particular subject topic, the academic method is one of "taking it or leaving it", either using what one reads for the purpose of an argument, or otherwise leaving it out of the argument by way of justifying commentary to this effect. In contradistinction to this academic method, the aim of a polemical essay in architecture theory is to take the texts that one finds and then manipulate them as one sees fit, for the explicit purpose of laying out a polemical trajectory of theory and subsequent further theory that is already emergent from the bowels of a particular pre-existent psycho-geography of the author. By doing so, the writing of architecture theory becomes approached in the model of an open-ended polemical essay, in parallel with the manner an activist, or in Guattari's words an "enthusiast", might work with texts that they find: to take what is found, manipulate it as seen fit for the purposes of "throwing light on present circumstances" and then leaving it once a consequential plane of thought is arrived at, or to which one is delivered through their manipulation and use of texts, in order for action to then find a new ground, and indeed a new praxis: that is to use texts as a vehicle for action. In this way, theoretical architectural speculation serves as a tool for directing a life and directing a research oeuvre toward the object of a particular concern. Such thinking through of architecture as a discipline and a practice cannot be done without recourse to thinking through and critiquing society from which architecture emerges and to which it is inexorably attached, and ultimately finds its way back to – the two facets of architecture and society must go hand-in-hand in the process of unfolding any theory about architecture.

It must be pointed out in this regard, that the taking of Guattari's quote for the purposes of an argument as evidenced here is of an academic method, living it out and putting it to use is of an activist method. As Henri Lefebvre has said of his own work in relation to *The Production of Space*, it had been "informed from beginning to end by a project... I refer to the project of a different society, a different mode of production"[28], which in the case of architecture theory aims to forward a condition where architecture "would be governed by different conceptual deter-minations"[29]. In so far as this has been achieved, architecture theory becomes an instrument for activism and a means toward a critical and creative praxis; it is this that provides promise to the possibility for architecture theory.

On Poetics, *Poiesis* and Architecture

Much has been written about and from within the philosophical turn in architecture in recent decades, beginning with Peter Eisenman and his Oppositions/Institute of Architecture and Urban Studies journal in the 1970s in relation to Structuralism, Bernard Tschumi, Peter Eisenman and others in relation to Deconstruction in the late-1980s, and more recently the Deleuzian turn in architecture in the 1990s surrounding Greg Lynn, Foreign Office Architects and Asymptote to mention just a few. In evaluating these excursions of architecture into philosophy – or might it be the other way around, of philosophy's excursions into architecture – one thing must not be forgotten, namely that "philosophy is directly concerned with universal truths"[1] whereas architecture is concerned more closely with a particular way of putting together, which is to say with poetry. Whilst philosophy addresses truth in relation to thought, "poetry's concern is indirect: the universality of poetry is a by-product of its aim to construct effective plots"[2]. Therefore a possibly more amiable approach to investigating possible different and novel ways of putting together, whilst keeping in mind the important strides that philosophical enquiry within the discipline of architecture has made in our recent past on architecture production, might be a turning toward the meaning of *poiesis* as a means to produce poetically.

To examine how architecture or an architectonics might be derivative of poetics, Aristotle's well-known text *Poetics* must be borrowed from and inflected toward an architectural interpretation. By following the instruction to devising good poetry in the form of tragedy, which Aristotle's *Poetics* deals with, a closer understanding of poetics in architecture and thus a particular way of putting together for the purposes of realizing *poiesis* in architecture might be had.

The first term with which Aristotle confronts us in with in the process of putting together poetics and realizing *poiesis* is the term *tekhnê*, which means craft, skill or the art of making something well. Poetics and with it a thoughtful and pleasant way of putting together something for the purposes of built realization resides in the meaning of the term *tekhnê*, which corresponds to a "productive capacity informed by an understanding of [something's] intrinsic rationale"[3]. To do poetics and achieve *poiesis*, and to do architecture thoughtfully, requires an intrinsic understanding of the act of making, and beyond that an intrinsic understanding of the outcomes of such made space's occupation and habitation, which intrinsic understanding results in something being put together thoughtfully, intelligently and well, whether derivative of a philosophically inflected inquiry or otherwise. Such thoughtful and well devised putting together in architecture does not necessarily need to abandon philosophical thought on possible approaches to architecture (and even might also reinforce such philosophical inquiry through addressing how construction and materiality has a relation to representation for instance), but nonetheless requires to work with *percept* as much as with truth, or at least alongside it, to realize an outcome of poetic form.

To put something together well, to make something poetically, is the aim of poetics resulting in *poiesis*, and arguably the aim of architecture. Whilst harnessing truth toward the means of form through philosophy to inquire about how one might assemble something might indeed account for an outcome of *poiesis*, it requires beyond that an understanding of the entire palette of the means to producing poetics, as opposed to only or merely truth. Having said this, *poiesis* is as much the result of art, skill and craft as it is of an intelligently crafted and thought through structure of approach to a problem. The fact that "human beings produce, amongst other things, poems"[4] shows that human beings require beauty as much as truth, and it is in the production of beauty in the context of truth that *tekhnê* comes to fore.

The production of beauty is not some sort of aesthetic category as rather the accomplishment of thinking through something well, and executing it with craft, skill and art. Just as "human beings produce, amongst other things, poems", human beings also and equally produce, amongst other things, buildings and spaces, and the production of buildings and spaces too can be done poetically resulting in *poiesis*, which is to say with *tekhnê*.

Indeed, for architecture to be good, useful and beautiful, it must be executed through and with *tekhnê*. The reason for this is – and this is the entering of philosophical truth onto the terrain of architecture – that because just as with poems, intense pleasure and a feeling of well-being can be derived from well thought through buildings and spaces, that is to say from good architecture. So for good, useful and pleasurable architecture to be thought up and realized, the first requirement is that the architect possess *tekhnê* in relation to what s/he is focusing on and attempting to realize and execute, regardless of what might come to inform that *tekhnê*.

The second category of conception in Aristotle's *Poetics* beyond *tekhnê* toward realizing *poiesis* is *mimêsis*. Aristotle considers *mimêsis* not only a hallmark of good tragedy and thus of good poetry, but also of good painting. The argument for mimetic presence in the execution of poetry or painting is necessary for the purpose of evoking affect. It is the creation of affect within poetry through *mimêsis* that makes the poetry true to its desired genre, which is to say a tragedy. To argue for *mimêsis* and thus poetics in architecture is to argue for the presence of affects, and just as good forms of "both painting and poetry [are] forms of *mimêsis*"[5], the same *mimêsis* applicable to both painting and poetry must also be applicable to that other sphere of creative creation where *tekhnê* is required, namely architecture. Indeed the ability of architecture to evoke and

141

hence create affect, just like poetry in tragedy and in painting, is the first sign of it existing as architecture as such, and the evidence of *tekhnê* in its conception.

Malcolm Heath in his Introduction to the 1996 Penguin edition of Aristotle's *Poetics* states of *mimêsis*, that "an imitation need not be a straightforward copy of the object imitated; the similarity between the object and its likeness may reside in a more oblique and abstract correspondence (as the doctrine that music contains "likenesses" of states of character proves)"[6]. Indeed the Situationists in the 1960s would go one step further and deliberately invoke *mimêsis* distorted in order to create their affect of *detournement* in art and the urban landscape. However, while poetic classical Greek poetry achieves *mimêsis* or mimetic likeness of something evoking affect through an application of "rhythmical language, with or without melodic accompaniment"[7], architecture as *tekhnê* in which mimesis is used, must use a different form of imitation, one in which sensate effects creating affect have an opportunity to become apparent through either use, habitation or viewing. It is because mimetic affects are used, that an affect can come about in the user; and if those mimetic affects are furthermore distorted to create *detournements*, an even better affect of subjective alterity may be accomplished, and thus with it critical architecture as such.

Aristotle argues that, "...tragedy is composed in "language made pleasurable""[8]; architecture in order for it to be poetics and achieve *poiesis* must also be composed either of space made pleasurable thoughtfully, or alternatively and in parallel, of space made edifying through the creation of subjective alterity. It is poetics and the pursuit of *poiesis* which achieves this in architecture – be it of a critical nature or otherwise.

"Aristotle observes that imitation is naturally pleasurable to human beings, and explains this with reference to the process of recognition which it involves"[9]. This reference to "recognition" is the site of the affect, the site of the affect coming to presence and registering in the behavior, habitation or perception of the user or viewer. Without such creation of affect, architecture remains weak; whilst conversely with a deliberate creation of affect through *mimêsis*, architecture has the promise of becoming a strong medium of communication. The stronger the vessel of communication architecture might be, the greater registering of affects come to pass through it. In order for affects to come to pass and register upon the user, a mimetic quality is required, be it critical – or in other terms truthfully edifying – in nature or otherwise, and it is thus that the architecture enters poetics and achieves *poiesis*.

A further consideration in making architecture poetically is what Aristotle terms as plot in poetry. Aristotle argues that, "Poetry is better if it has a structured plot"[10], namely a structured and well thought through story to tell. Heath states that, "the importance of a coherently structured plot is a crucial element in The Poetics [of Aristotle]"[11], and just like poetry reliant on *tekhnê* for the bringing about of *poiesis*, architecture, too, can be argued to require a structured plot in order for its value to be apparent. The structured plot of architecture is found within its sharpness of *tekhnê*, which plays out through the relationship between function, context, form and resultant materiality and construction that accompanies the realization of that function within a given context.

Plot in architecture could be summarized by the process of thinking through the way toward realization of a building or space starting from the givens of the site. From the givens of the site emerges context, which context comes to inflect upon concept, that is the ideas generative of materiality, construction and form for a given site in the context of its intended use. Plot is thus an amalgamation of the entire process of architectural thinking based on context, concept and resultant content. The intrinsic links between context, concept and resultant content of that which becomes realized through architecture is the mark of a plot's *poiesis*, and of the architecture of the space-making being done thoughtfully, interestingly and well – even possibly critically.

Thus, just like poetics producing good tragedy, the architectural poetics of plot "consists of a *connected* series of events: one thing follows on another as a necessary consequence"[12], which involves the process of iterative thinking between context, concept and resultant content. "Secondly, the plot consists of a self-contained series of events"[13], which is to say that the thinking between and leading from context to concept to resultant content is iterative and self-reflexive, always moving between each in the course of its realization by way of material or resultant behavior in the outcome of use. An architecturally inflected reading of Aristotle's thoughts on plot thus consist of a connected series of considerations between context, concept, form, desired behavioral outcomes and function. It is the realization of this careful consideration between context, concept, form, desired behavioral outcomes, resultant perceptions and function that demonstrates the measure of *tekhnê* of the architect and the measure of *poiesis* in his/her resultant architecture.

Thus *poiesis* comes about in the built environment as a result of the careful consideration between context, concept, form, desired behavioral outcomes, resultant perceptions and function, and as such "it is the *plot*, [which is to say] the underlying sequence of actions, that [produces] this structure"[14], which is to say a particular type and condition of desired result. The plot in architecture is the process by which the function is realized in the context of concept and site, and what surrounds the site. This process is structured, and the structure of this process is the realization of architecture, similarly to how the plot and its structure of sequence of actions results in the realization of good poetic tragedy. Such outcome might be realized through a philosophically inflected inquiry or otherwise.

Aristotle speaks of the unity of plot in classical Greek tragedy.

A unity might be said to be something complete and whole. The poetic unity of a realized building or space is the completeness and wholeness of its function coupled with its sensate and behavioral affects, with the two working together and reciprocally on one another in the context of use, producing in turn through that context of use a particular reading and behavioral and perceptual outcome.

> In judging the quality of one [...] plot over against the another, it is their emotional impact to which Aristotle appeals. He identifies two things which make a sequence of events particularly effective: "These effects occur above all when things come about contrary to expectation, but because of one another"[15].

Thus a plot that creates affect through contrary expectations but because of one another is a plot that creates interesting sensate and behavioral affects in the user. It is these interesting sensate and behavioral affects that come to be read and which come to register on the use of a space, giving it character and a particular nature. As such, the creation of a particular character and nature of space in the context of function is what arguably must be termed as architecture. Doing it well, which is to say thinking through a "...a well-formed plot [...is] in principle [what] poetry ought to aim for"[16].

We can thus state from such architecturally inflected reading of the role of the plot in Aristotle's *Poetics* that "...there is an intimate connection between the cohesion of the plot and the emotional impact at which [poetics] aims"[17]. In architecture done with poetics achieving *poiesis* just like in the poetics of good tragedy, there is an intimate connection between the cohesion of the plot, or in another term "the realization and resolution of the architectural process", and the emotional and intellectual impact that a realized architectural space creates.

Another element of good poetics based on Aristotle's discussion of tragedy is the creation of a particular *hamartia*, or what might be translatable to English as character. In classical Greek tragedy, *hamartia* (character) is created through a distinct and obvious error in moral or intellectual content of a leading protagonist in the course of the story, producing an error of expectation and an element of surprise in the viewer.

A deliberate and obvious error or a series of juxtaposed deliberate and obvious seeming "errors" creating a deviation from what might be expected can also create a particular type of character in a conceived space. Deliberate and obvious "errors" that might be incorporated into the resolution of architecture momentarily suspend the user's expectations of the relationship between behavior and function or between perception and function, producing in term an element of surprise, an element of the unexpected. Such elements of surprise and of the unexpected create a particular type of uncanny character in the resultant architecture and in its use, which errors might stem from a deliberate and particular consideration in the process of working out the plot. Errors done well thus become actors in architecture of difference and of otherness, and ultimately a realization of subjective alterity in the course of the space's inhabitation. In classical Greek tragedy, character "is imitated when what is said or (presumably) done reveals the nature of the choice that is made, and hence the underlying moral disposition of the person speaking or acting"[18]. In architecture, character is created as a result of an expectation of the user being realized differently, or perhaps not being realized at all. The creation of architecture incorporating such "errors" and the nature and type of errors arise from the libidinal lines that course through an architect, depending on what function or perception of function s/he wants to create alterity in. An incorporation of "errors" arising from libidinal lines is nothing else than the voicing of the architect's desire and particular disposition to serving and then solving a problem of function, perception, behavioral outcome or form in the course of realizing a given architecture of space.

A further consideration in the creating of *poiesis* in Aristotle's *Poetics* is the attainment of *katharsis*. In tragedy, *katharsis* results by way of "effecting through pity and fear the purification of [...] emotions"[19]. In architecture, *katharsis* is achieved as a result of what becomes conceived, drawn and realized fitting well within the context and within its function, whilst drawing-in the user or viewer into a particular set of sensate and behavioral affects. *Katharsis* in architecture might be defined as how well a space functions, or how well and interestingly it relates to its context by either reinforcing its characteristics or suspending them, and thus producing as a result sensate affects in and upon the users. Ultimately, *katharsis* in architecture produces a "...relief that brings, [or creates something that] is pleasurable"[20].

"For Aristotle the crucial point is [...] to feel the right degree of emotion (or pleasure) in the right circumstances"[21], this is what the sensate affect of *katharsis* is in architecture, and which an architectural realization should aim for. *Katharsis* might happen at the point of turning an angle onto a different part of function within the space, or at the threshold of entry or exit, or in the choice and application of materiality or construction techniques, or in the architecture of illumination and play of light, or in the texture and color of a given space, be it in daylight or at night. Furthermore *katharsis* might be able to be achieved in the fixtures and fittings of a space and how they are designed to be used. *Katharsis* thus could be understood and inflected for the purposes of architecture as the resolution of excessive disorder or equally of the disordering of excessive order, which will not be born out of the same process in every instance, but requires a careful thinking through of desired sensate affects that the architect wishes to create, and will correspond to the degree of appropriateness the architecture conveys to each user in turn.

If poetics can be defined as composition in verse[22] and a

particular composition of that verse, then the poetics of architecture could be defined as composition in material and a particular type of composition in material within the context of site and its type inflected by concepts, or of what type is hoped to be achieved consequent to having first conceived something for a site and then executed it in built form and realized through it some intention.

If "poetry is concerned with particular sequences of events, [with] the connection between those events mean[ing] that they instantiate universal structures"[23], then the architectural process is also concerned with a particular sequence of events, in such a way as that which is thought up to be realized instantiates universal experiences of sensate affects. The sum effect of *tekhnê*, *mimêsis*, plot, *hamartia* (character) and resultant *katharsis* is what we call *poiesis*, and in its architecturally inflected understanding, a poetics of architecture.

On the Significance of Corners

A corner is the point where one or more straight lines change direction.

As a result of the straight line changing direction, a diversion is born.

In consequence to the diversion of the line, an angle is also born between the former straight line and the subsequent straight line.

A corner can also be formed of planes in accordance with the above description.

A corner thus becomes both the respective beginning and end of two straight lines or planes.

A corner therefore marks both a beginning and an end.

As a result of a corner, two dimensionality begets the prospect of being marked out.

Corners are the prospect of two dimensionality.

Whilst the corner diverges only one line, two dimensionality is the only ensuing prospect.

When the corner, however, diverges into two subsequent lines, three dimensionality is born as a result of the two divergent axes and the original third line.

Corners with three axes are thus the prerequisite for spatial representation, and the beginning of the possibility of architecture.

Corners are the prerequisite of architecture, and their inalienable component.

Corners are what enable architecture to occur.

Without corners, which is to say without a change of direction of a line, architecture can not emanate.

Corners thus mark out the beginning possibility of ensuing architecture.

In thinking of the corner as the beginning of something, it is more prominent than what follows it precisely because it is the beginning of something.

In thinking of the corner as the end of something, it is more prominent than what preceded it, precisely because it is the end of something.

Corners are therefore prominent.

Because corners are prominent, they require careful consideration.

Corner areas on buildings require thoughtful treatment precisely because of their prominence.

Corner positions on streets and thoroughfares thus also require thoughtful treatment precisely because of their prominence.

A corner divides two directions. The division happens at the respective lines' intersection, thus marking out the corner.

In the intersection of two lines occurring, an Event happens, which creates the corner.

The corner beyond being prominent is also thus an Event.

As an Event, the corner should be marked or molded by the lines, multiplicities and assemblages that make up both lines or in cases planes that come to intersect at its occurrence. It is in this way that the corner remains truthful to what precedes it.

The content of the corner is thus always pre-established, if often hidden.

The pre-established content of the corner resides within the content of the lines or planes that come to create it and that it resolves.

The corner is thus fulsome, and because of this it is expressive, even if only simple.

Corners are expressive because they carry and resolve the content of adjoining lines or planes.

Because corners carry and resolve the content of adjoining lines or planes, they are important.

It is because corners are important that we begin the

foundation of a building with a ceremonial "corner stone".

It is on such stone and on the position of such stone that the foundation of what is to follow rests.

The corner is thus both a foundation, which is to say a beginning point, as well as a resolution, which is to say an end point.

Corners are the alpha and the omega of both plane and of architecture.

Special head thus should be paid to corners and their resolution.

As such, corners become marking points.

Corners mark our territory.

Corners mark out and contain or exclude space.

A joining up of corner points creates a plane or a volume resulting in a final corner where the joining up becomes complete.

The area or space defined by corners thus contain.

A plane is marked by having corners.

A volume is thus also marked by having corners (even if curved), which mark its limit.

Corners therefore define a limit position.

In defining a limit position, corners define what is inside or what is outside.

Corners belong both to the inside (what they define to contain), and to the outside (what they exclude)

Corners are thus located on the division between outside and inside, depending on whether they define a convex or concave relation to the rest of the space.

Corners can thus also exclude things.

In corners we place things.

Corners are highlighted and defined by what we place in them.

Corners give prominence to that which is placed in them.

For this reason also, corners are special and important.

The properly defined geometric condition of a corner is a point.

From the point of the corner, lines or planes emanate.

If a corner is a series of conjoining points in a linear sequence, it is defined as a line that might be an edge.

If a corner is a series of conjoining points defined by an origo point or points, it is defined as a curve.

In some instances a corner can be curved prior to giving way to lines or planes, which they themselves could be curved or straight.

Corners form the essence of geometry.

If a corner is equal to 360 degrees, it ceases to be a corner and becomes a circle or a sphere.

If a corner is less than 360 degrees, all of the above mentioned points hold true to it.

Woe to him or her who neglects to think through or pay attention to the articulation of corners or a corner.

It is thus, that corners might begin to be thought in fact.

The Voice of Ruins

He disembarked in a living room without chairs or gilt
moldings:
just rotting beams, vases with plastic flowers, windows
whose broken panes looked out onto the highway. No wind,
no sea: only the sound of cars entering through the cracks
to echo on the ceiling (rafters showing through the stucco
remains). Outside he hung onto the rusted rails
of decrepit balconies. He discerned, through the underbrush
that was overrunning everything, a landscape worthy
of a Romantic painting. The houses covering the valley and
the hills taken over by scrap iron hide a past
with flocks and shepherds. But perhaps the flute's song
was never heard here. Indeed, this house conserves nothing
but ancient silences, which the using has transformed
into sepia
spots in memory. Now they're blended into the color
of the walls
and harbor only dens of scarcely discernable reptiles,
in winter, hidden from the universe. But someone was here
very recently. And a pile of wood still smokes as
the sun ascends from the horizon, where dawns cold colors
do not dissipate, and no bird greets
the new day.
Nuno Júdice, Meditation on Ruins (translated from the Portuguese by Richard Zenith)

Nuno Júdice's poem "Meditations on Ruins" speaks of the vulnerability of architecture, of all that remains of it once habitation and function give way to "broken panes", "rotting beams" and the still silence of the dawn. The house that is depicted in the poem once presumably housed laughter, joy and life in abundance; now only "ancient silences" remain to be contemplated "where dawn's cold colors do not dissipate".

Such is the vulnerability of stone, steel and wood. The French have a word that entertains the immovability of architecture, namely that of *immeuble*, translatable to mean that which is "unmovable", the solid, the permanent. The "unmovable", the solid, the permanent may well be so while function is being exercised, but once function ceases, the seeming eternity of *immeuble* gives way to weeds and the wind and the rain, only to turn that which was thought of as permanent into wreckage: such is architecture.

Indeed, in contemplating architecture and its nature, an interesting intersection can be found at the junction of the terms "function" and "permanence". Permanence only prevails whilst function remains intact. Once function is lost or altered, re-articulated or changed, the immovability of the stone, steel and timber which housed that function also becomes lost. Function is thus the preserve of the *immeuble*.

In contemplating these introductory remarks, I wish to ruminate on that which comes of architecture once function ceases or is removed from that which was initially conceived as "unmovable" or *immeuble*. In other words, I wish to entertain the ultimate role of architecture, which role can be found in the sentiment of Nuno Júdice's poem, namely a meditation on the voice of ruins. In having said that, it is not only architecture of the material kind this essay will muse on, but also the architecture of a life.

That a built architectural structure's function eventually ceases or becomes rearticulated from what was originally conceived for use is verifiable in almost all, if not all creations of masonry, steel and timber. Masonry seems to us as the very embodiment of the "unmovable", "the permanent", "the solid", the *"immeuble"*. But the placing of masonry for the purposes of housing function, its lines and right-angles defining as they do spaces for the production of activity and purpose is nothing other than the production of place: once activity and purpose changes or ceases, the lines and right-angles of the masonry, the timber or the steel lose their purpose and efficacy. Indeed "placing" as an act of architecture, as an act of conceiving space loses its efficacy once function becomes evacuated. This is what has become of all the monuments and constructions of the ancients as a result of time passing and function and purpose being lost, be it the Parthenon in Athens, or the Hagia Sophia in Istanbul to name but two examples.

If we consider the European continent and its built environment, most of that which has been constructed and is still in use and functioning, is no more than 800 years old – the oldest of which would be the Gothic cathedrals from the 1220s onwards – the early-mid thirteenth century – whilst the vast majority of the Continent's built fabric is no more than 150 to 200 years old. Anything older than 800 years is mostly ruin or has been demolished, such as most of the built environment of the Dark Ages and that of the Roman Imperium before it, with only the odd Romanesque church bearing witness to a former age. Indeed invariably where structures as old as these have remained, their function has also remained intact, most obviously so the ecclesiastic ceremonies associated with the Roman church. Architecture therefore is not "unmovable", but ends up in the most part being demolished or falling into decay, with at most ruins to show for a once flourishing purpose, but with the function having been evacuated.

Such contemplation of all that is conceived to be built is a rather sobering exercise. Architects conceive of their work as that which is *"immeuble"*, that which remains forever in the permanency of its materiality, defining a use and purpose to its spaces as a making of place for eternity if you will. With the passing of time, however, purpose and function also changes. With the passing of time sacred rights of the initiated lapse and pass into memory, the stone and steel and masonry lose their purpose of placing. Once materiality loses its purpose of placing through wear and tear or through the loss of purpose and function, the materiality in question also loses its purpose, only to become a relic of a bygone age.

The architect Sir John Soane conceived of his creations and indeed his whole life's work in just such hope of permanence. We read in Christopher Woodward's evocative title *In Ruins*, that, "[Soane] having no deep religious conviction, [...] based his hopes of immortality on architecture. And yet architecture [is] so flimsy..."[1] Such is the vulnerability of a person who attempts to base his hopes of immortality in materiality, especially that of the architectural kind.

It must be apt to be voiced, that architects should be under no illusion: the vast majority of their work, if not almost its totality for most – bar that which becomes preserved as ruin – will ultimately cease to exist and cease to be remembered; and even that which preserves as ruin becomes a haunt of memory, a haunt of function and purpose lost. Having said this, however, the practice and product of the profession of architecture is still nonetheless more enduring than the professions of law and medicine, in the case of law that might have a lifespan of maybe a few hundred years, whilst medicine is tied to the fate of the mortality of the patient, sometimes measurable in months, at most a number of decades from the medical procedure performed. Architecture in comparison to the longevity of the product of these other two professions is indeed more enduring, but in no way everlasting, let alone eternal.

What then can be said therefore of architecture as a measure of the *immeuble*?

The enduring epochal legacy or value of architecture, precisely because it is destined to decay and destruction, is found ultimately in that which survives its total destruction and passes from physicality and memory, namely architecture as ruin. In the words of Woodward, "I want to tell them that a ruin has two values. It has an objective value as an assemblage of brick and stone, and it has a subjective value as an inspiration to artists"[2]. It is this which is architecture's ultimate value and nothing much beside.

The ultimate function and voice of that which is conceived as *immeuble*, is encapsulated by Woodward again thus: "To the lover of the ruinous [...] the attraction is in the sight of transience and vulnerability"[3]. The ultimate purpose therefore of architecture and the built environment is found in the meaning that the passing of time conveys upon it, namely its voicing of the meaning of transience, vulnerability, futility and memory. It is in this voicing and in this evocation of memory that its ultimate purpose is found, and its ultimate presence enabled.

The fact that this is so is that "a building can seem more beautiful in ruins than when its original design is intact"[4], which is to say that the meaning of transience in life, the voicing of life's vulnerability and ultimate loss and decay, the ultimate futility of our lives in most part as echoed by ruins is the ultimate beauty that architecture can convey. This is so, because it is in time having passed that "a ruin [becomes] a dialogue between an incomplete reality and the imagination of the spectator"[5], creating a voicing of meaning that speaks of the futility of actions, the meaninglessness of permanence, the vacuity of the *immeuble*, and the ultimate reign of memory through time, and only of memory. It is memory and what the past conveys to us in the present that has any ultimate meaning for our lives, and which can edify us in our conduct – the production of memory and the evocation of edification is the ultimate cornerstone of all architecture and production of built function; it is for this reason the ruin is the ultimate beauty and purpose of architecture and the built environment.

Woodward goes on to write that, "The first attraction of architectural decay is [the] seductive stillness..."[6], or what we might call "spiritual desolation"[7]. It is in this spiritual desolation, where function and purpose have come to cease that the lines and right-angles of our masonry and steel constructions reveal their most meaningful act: the voicing of memory, the voicing of time having passed, and thus the voicing of ultimate meaning and a revealing of the condition and flow of life.

Such is life and such is architecture. Without ruins, without decay, without the splendor of spiritual desolation, would we be able to ultimately learn or conceive anything about our own transience? Without ruins, without function and purpose lost and having been evacuated, could we possibly reflect on our own transient nature? It is the transience of architecture in the form of ruin which echoes the meaning and futility of life to us, and which courses through generation upon generation as an edifying echo.

In reflecting on these comments, indeed we might say that it is not only the built fabric of cities and buildings that give way to time and upon which time's sway registers, but indeed:

> *All our works fall and sicken,*
> *Nothing is eternal:*
> *The Colossei die, the Baths,*
> *The worlds are dust, their pomp nothing...*[8]
> Salvator Rosa

These are the words of seventeenth century Italian poet and painter Salvator Rosa, and well we might say, it is the sentiment of decay and ruin and what that might speak to us as encapsulated in these lines which we remember of his work. Again memory and time, time passing and futility, meaning, purpose and function.

"In ruins movement is halted, and Time suspended"[9]. In ruins memory is found of past actions, of past lives of past flow, of past life. In ruins an edifying is found of futility and of the vulnerability of life. In writing these sober sentiments one is reminded of Diderot's review of the 1767 salon in Paris where numerous sketches of ruin-scapes were exhibited by Chauteaubriand on his return from his *Grand Tour* of Italy, of which he wrote: "Everything vanishes, everything perishes, everything passes away; the world alone remains, time alone continues"[10].

In the sketches of ruins and in the actual perception of material ruins "time is suspended, or reversed, or erased...."[11], "the hand of Time"[12] is made known to the spectator and the contemplator. Indeed to know time, to know passing, and to come face-to-face with the flow of life one need only contemplate a ruin. In contemplating a ruin one perceives the "hand of time", that nothing, not even the seemingly *immeuble* and that which was conceived as *immeuble* can withstand the flow of time. It is indeed the flow of time that we witness when contemplating a ruin, the flow of time which has passed and left behind all the haughty aspirations of the building's maker, for only time, the passing of time and futility to speak of her ambition.

> When we contemplate ruins, we contemplate our own future. To statesmen, ruins predict the fall of Empires, and to philosophers the futility of mortal man's aspirations. To a poet, the decay of a monument represents the dissolution of the individual ego in the flow of Time; to a painter or architect, the fragments of a stupendous antiquity call into question the purpose of their art. Why struggle with a brush or chisel to create beauty of wholeness when far greater works have been destroyed by Time?[13]

Everything is ultimately destroyed by time except ruins – and it is in this exception that the profession of architecture might find its solace. In escaping time and the flow of time, the ruin becomes the marker of a dialogue, a dialogue with the past. It is because the ruin might speak so to say of the past, of ambitions past, of function and purpose and life past, that it has any meaning at all. The meaning and relevance of the ruin – and thus of architecture that survives to its ultimate state and condition as ruin – is found precisely in this meaning and relevance. The meaning and relevance of architecture through its ultimate form the ruin is found in the dialogue it might have with a future spectator. In this sense not all purpose is lost. The function may be lost, the life, the joy, the laughter, the purpose of the original structure may be lost and fallen into decay; however, what remains that escapes the ultimate futility of conceiving of a life of steel, timber and masonry construction is the promise of dialogue one's work might enable with the future. It is in this promise of a dialogue that architecture and the ruin find some efficacy.

Alas, efficacy and promise for the profession of architecture and the work of the person of the architect may well be found, but only in decay. And because it is only in decay and in ruin, it is not the building *per sé* that communicates, but the time encapsulated in the ruin, the time encapsulated of a bygone era, of bygone life, and a bygone condition of civilization. So in effect the ruin robs the architect of all intention and perceived grandeur, to convey not the architecture nor the intentions of the architect, but time, time passing and past civilization.

The role of architecture and the architect is then to realize that all his/her creations will come to ruin, and it is in the conveying of a time in history, of the time of conception of the building with all its function and purpose that s/he is called to. The architect and his/her building are called to act as a time-machine between the past and the present, or between the present and the future, with the building in question acting as a communication vessel of time passed. It is this that is the ultimate purpose, promise and only possibility of architecture in the long run.

But isn't all our conception and action in life such? Is it not apt to say that:

It is thus [through the ruin, through what the ruin embodies] that we are warned at each step of our nothingness; [when] man goes to meditate on the ruins of empires; he forgets that he is himself a ruin still more unsteady, and that he will fall before these remains do.[14]

Woodward quoting Chateaubriand from his *Génie du Christianisme.*

Be a person an architect or alternatively of a building occupation or not, it is this that ruins ultimately convey and communicate to us, namely that all conception and action, all will and glory pass, just as time passes, to but return in a moment of contemplative mood on past edifices by people in the future.

The ruin is therefore a metaphor for life, not just of the life of the architect and his/her conceptions, but of all life and all action and conception therein. The ruin is the beacon that communicates the frailty of man, and this because time, and with it each individual as living within and as a part of time passes. When we contemplate past actions, past lives, buildings fallen into decay and ruinous, lives lived and lost, isn't this what we really perceive: the fate of all life and of living? Thus "ruins become a popular metaphor for the decay of an individual life"[15], be that life of an individual involved in the building professions or otherwise, indeed all Men.

Architecture therefore does have a purpose, and that is to communicate as a beacon to the future Man's futility. It is this which is the purpose of all action conceived and executed, namely that all is futile, all things pass, all things decay, whether of greatness or of humble ordinariness. In this act of decay and passing we are all brought to the same level, we are leveled together to a plane of memory in which and through which a beacon for edifying the living is erected. It is this which is the meaning of all life, be it wondrous or ordinary; it is in what we are capable in contributing to dialogue with the future, with those who come after us that our lives find meaning and our actions find purpose. The only solace left to us in our own meaning and action is the momentary satisfaction and happiness they might impart to us while we are living, and that but for a moment: such is architecture.

The function of the ruin is therefore of a specter or ghosts, be it the ruin of a building or of actions and achievements in life. Whatever we come to accomplish in life, its true meaning is what echoes forth from it as a haunting to the living. Ruins, be it of a material variety or of other variety thus embody a haunting; ruins of past life act as "a troop of ghosts"[16], teaching, communicating to, entering into dialogue with, edifying those who come after us. It is this which is the ultimate and only possible purpose of all our actions: to speak to the future, whether near or distant.

It is this speaking to the future whether near or distant that our lives' "...genius [is] germinated [by] in the damp shadows of ancient decay"[17] only to become a specter, a haunting, a voice for future lives. Thus ruins as a metaphor for life do not escape total silence – indeed none of our lives escape total silence, but on the contrary have the ability and promise to act as a beacon, to act as a voice that comes to illuminate minds and deeds of the future. It is in this metaphor that the promise and grandeur of life might be found, and in this metaphor alone – but always accompanied by the whisper of the futility of that grandeur in equal measure.

Ruins thus enable a reflection on life, as well as a realization, a coming to terms with life's futility. Life must therefore be seen as an "absurd" flow, following the thought of Albert Camus. Ruins enact a realizing that becomes the mark of the beginning of real genius in lives yet to be lived or being lived, and it is only when ruins are so realized that creativity commences and with it the possibility for beauty, whether that may be concerning the object of architecture, of literature or that of the fullness of life. It is only when one has exhausted everything, all function, all purpose, all habitation, including every ounce of prospect in significance, that real creation, real thought has the prospect to protrude into being, and even then it is not certain it will do so. It is this which is the meaning uttered by the voice of ruins.

> When reactor number four at the Chernobyl Nuclear Power Plant exploded in 1986 the result was the worst nuclear accident in history. Large areas of Ukraine, Belarus and Russia were severely contaminated, requiring the evacuation and resettlement of over 336,000 people. Pripyat, one kilometer from the reactor, was designed as an exemplar of Soviet planning for the 50,000 people who worked at the power plant.[18]

From this segment of text that accompanied a photo-exhibition held at the Architectural Association, School of Architecture, in London in 2011, we realize that not even the mighty edifices of empires last. Just as the Roman Imperium and the Holy Roman Empire only left behind vestiges of their glory, so too today in our current time of recent past, the town of Pripyat, which served the nuclear power station in Chernobyl and its workers, will be one of the few remaining edifices left to posterity of Soviet glory. The ideology, the achievements of social and industrial significance will with time fade; what will speak of Soviet glory will be the ruins of Pripyat and the reading they convey of life under Soviet Socialism. For this, and only for this, they are of significance, for it is because of this role that future generations will be able to understand something about social mechanisms, everyday life, work-leisure structure and consumables. The ruin will thus speak, the ruin will thus edify.

Whether one considers a settlement such as Pripyat, or an individual building, or a collection of monuments together with buildings such as those found in ancient Babylon, Memphis, Athens, Troy, Mycenae, Rome or Carthage, or that of an individual's or society's life, the one thing that their builders and their builders' lives have achieved is the leaving behind of ruin. It is through these ruins that we can glimpse an insight into daily life, into economic life, into political life, into household life and into other spheres of existence, and learn from these spheres of existence for the countenance of our own lives. This is the purpose of all life: to become ruin; and in ruin will life be glorified.

In regards to our own time, and in regards to our own life and conduct, may we rightly say in the words of Hungarian poet George Faludy:

And won't this Age of ours, up to its neck
in steel and concrete cities where we work
so avidly, though aimlessly, be damned
by a bright posterity as The Dark?
George Faludy, The Desert, 1941 (12th stanza)

Might we also rightly say in the words of Vitruvius that architecture is the mother of all arts, and remind ourselves that to live well is art; might we couple this with the words of Oscar Wilde that "all art is quite useless"[19].

References

Preface

1 Adam Ferguson, *An Essay on the History of Civil Society*, 1767, (ed.) Duncan Forbes, Edinburgh University Press, 1966, p217. – as quoted in Lynn Hunt, *Measuring Time – Making History*, CEU Press, Budapest-New York, 2008, p59.

The Discipline of Architecture and the Architectural Process

1 discipline and – disciple, from the *Chambers Dictionary of Etymology*, Chambers Harrap Publishers Ltd, London, 2012, p282.

2 Iain Sinclair, *Blake's London – the topographical sublime*, Swedenborg Society, London, 2012, p3.

3 Herbert Marcuse, *A Study on Authority*, Verso Books, London, 2008, Introduction, p7.

4 Ibid., p7.

5 Andrew Benjamin, *Architectural Philosophy*, The Athlone Press, London, 2000 – see chapter titled "Time, function and alterity in architecture".

6 Vitruvius, *The Ten Books on Architecture*, MH Morgan (translator), Harvard University Press, Cambridge, MA.,1914, p5.

Parkour and Architecture

1 Jan Witfeld, Ilona Gerling, Alexander Pach., *The Ultimate Parkour & Freerunning Book*, Mayer & Mayer Sport Ltd., Maidenhead, 2011., p26.

2 See Deleuze and Guattari, *Capitalism and Schizophrenia – A Thousand Plateaus*, Chapter 14., The Athlone Press, London, 1996.

3 Ibid., p.474.

4 Ibid., p.474-475.

Architecture as Politics

1   Hannah Arendt, *The Human Condition*, The University of Chicago Press, Chicago and London, 1998, p207-208.

2   Ibid., p.25.

3   Ibid., p.26.

4   Ibid., p.180.

5   Ibid., p.208.

6   This is not a direct quote from Arendt, but rather a paraphrasing of the sentiment behind her concept of *"vita activa"*. To read more on the concept of *vita activa* see chapters V and VI in Hannah Arendt, *The Human Condition*, The University of Chicago Press, Chicago-London, 1998.

7   Hannah Arendt, *The Human Condition*, The University of Chicago Press, Chicago and London, 1998, p.323.

8   Ibid., p.23.

9   Ibid., p.299.

10 Ibid., p.299.

Politics, Architecture and Activism

1   Peter Eisenman, "The Affects of Singularity", in *Architecture Design* Vol. 62 / No.11-12, Nov-Dec 1992, p.43.

2   Ibid., p.45.

3   Ibid., p.45.

4   Ibid., p.45.

5   For the four laws of Detournement, see Guy Debord and Gil J Wolman, "Methods of Detournement", in Ken Knabb (edited and translated) *Situationist International Anthology*, Bureau of Public Secrets, Berkeley CA, 1989, p.10-11.

6   See http://www.absoluteastronomy.com/topics/Detournement

7   Peter Eisenman, "The Affects of Singularity", in *Architecture Design* Vol. 62 / No.11-12, Nov-Dec 1992, p.45.

8   Ibid., p.45.

9   Bernard Tschumi, interview in *'K'* supplement magazine of

Kathimerini newspaper, 30/09/07

10 Hannah Arendt, *The Human Condition*, The University of Chicago Press, Chicago and London, 1998, p.9.

11 Ibid., p.9.

12 Ibid., p.9.

13 Ibid., p.9.

14 Ibid., p.9.

15 Ibid., p.188.

16 Ibid., p.188.

17 Ibid., p.188.

18 Ibid., p.188.

19 Andrew Benjamin, *Architectural Philosophy*, The Athlone Press, New Brunswick NJ, 2000, p.7.

20 Jean-Francois Lyotard, *Libidinal Economy*, Continuum, London, 1993, p.44.

21 Hannah Arendt, *The Human Condition*, The University of Chicago Press, Chicago and London, 1998, p.297.

22 Marcos Novak, Interview with Knut Mork, 1995, as viewed at http://www.altx.com/int2/marcos.novak.html on 10 February 2011.

23 see Marcos Novak – interview with Knut Mork, 1995, http://www.altx.com/int2/marcos.novak.html

24 Carlos Villanueva Brandt, *London + 10 - AA Agendas 10*, AA Publications, London, 2010.

25 Hannah Arendt, *The Human Condition*, The University of Chicago Press, Chicago and London, 1998, p.300.

26 see Victor Hugo, *The Hunchback of Notre Dame*, Chapter II – 'This Will Kill That'

The Promise of the Politics of Digital Architecture

1 Bernard Tschumi, interview in 'K' supplement magazine of *Kathimerini* newspaper, 30/09/07

2 Felix Guattari, "Les machines architecturales de Shin Takamatsu", in *Perspecta 42*, MIT Press, 28 February 2010,

    p.135.

3   Ibid., p.135.

4   Simone Brott, *Architecture for a free Subjectivity*, Ashgate, Farnham Surrey, 2011, p.91.

5   Ibid., p.119.

6   Jane Rendell et. al (ed.), *Critical Architecture*, Introduction, Routledge, Abingdon, 2007, p.7.

7   Felix Guattari, "Subjectivities: for Better or for Worse" in Gary Genosko (ed.) *The Guattari Reader*, Cambridge MA, Blackwell Publishers Ltd, 1996, p. 202.

8   Ibid., p.202.

9   Michel Foucault, *Madness and Civilisation*, Tavistock, London, 1967, p.vi.

A Reading of Planonemons

1   Gilles Deleuze, and Felix Guattari, *What is Philosophy?*, Verso, London, 1994, p.35-36.

2   Ibid., p.36.

3   Jacques Derrida, "Point de Folie – Maintenant l'architecture", in *Architecture Theory since 1968*, K. Michael Hays (ed.), Cambridge MA, MIT Press, 2000, p.573-574.

4   Peter Eisenman, an Architectural Design interview by Charles Jencks, *Architectural Design*, Vol. 58. 3-4, Wiley-Academy, London, 1988.

5   Peter Eisenman, "Architecture and the Problem of the Rhetorical Figure", in *Theorising a New Agenda for Architectural Theory*, Kate Nesbitt (ed.), Princeton Architectural Press, New York, 1996, p.176.

6   Ibid., p.177.

7   Ibid., p.178.

8   Ibid., p.178.

9   Ibid., p.180.

10   Ibid., p.180.

11   Gilles Deleuze, and Felix Guattari, *What is Philosophy?*, Verso,

London, 1994, p.40.

12   Ibid., p.39.

13   Peter Eisenman, "Moving Arrows, Eros and Other Errors", *AA Files #12*, AA Publications, London, 1986, p.77.

14   Ibid., p.77.

15   Jacques Derrida and Peter Eisenman, *Chora L Works*, The Monacelli Press, New York, 1997, p.7.

16   Ibid., p.10.

17   Ibid., p.8.

18   Ibid., p.35.

19   Ibid., p.10.

20   Ibid., p.33.

21   Gilles Deleuze, and Felix Guattari, *What is Philosophy?*, Verso, London, 1994, p.21.

22   Jacques Derrida and Peter Eisenman, *Chora L Works*, The Monacelli Press, New York, 1997, p.46.

23   Gilles Deleuze, and Felix Guattari, *What is Philosophy?*, Verso, London, 1994, p.24.

24   Ibid., p.24.

25   Ibid., p.24.

26   Ibid., p.5.

27   Ibid., p.32-33.

28   Ibid., p.51.

29   See Bernard Tschumi's *Event Cities II*, MIT Press, Cambridge MA, 2001.

30   See Peter Eisenman's essay "Moving Arrows, Eros and Other Errors", *AA Files #12*, AA Publications, London, 1986.

31   For a detailed description of the process of scaling in the design process of the garden see *Chora L Works*, transcript 5, The Monacelli Press, New York, 1997.

32   Jacques Derrida and Peter Eisenman, *Chora L Works*, The Monacelli Press, New York, 1997, p.80.

33   Jacques Derrida, "Why Peter Eisenman Writes such Good Books", in *Chora L Works*, The Monacelli Press, New York,

1997, p.96.

34 Ibid., p.221.

35 Gilles Deleuze, and Felix Guattari, *What is Philosophy?*, Verso, London, 1994, p.197.

36 Ibid., p.197.

37 Ibid., p.198.

38 Ibid., p.198.

39 Peter Eisenman, "The End of the Classical, The End of the Beginning, The End of the End", in *Architecture Theory since 1968*, Michael Hays (ed.), Cambridge MA, MIT Press, 2000, p.222.

40 Gilles Deleuze, and Felix Guattari, *What is Philosophy?*, Verso, London, 1994, p.217.

41 Ibid., p.218.

The Path on which Architecture Finds Itself

1 Jacques Derrida, "Architecture Where Desire May Live" (Architetture ove il desiderio puo abitare), *Domus*, 1986, p.671.

2 Deleuze and Guattari, *Capitalism and Schizophrenia – A Thousand Plateaus*, The Athlone Press, London, 1996, p.262-263.

3 Ibid., p.262-263.

4 Bernard Tschumi, *Event Cities 3*, MIT Press, Cambridge MA, 2004 – see Introduction.

5 Jean-Francois Lyotard, *Libidinal Economy*, Continuum, London, 1974.

6 Jean Baudrillard, *Mass, Identity, Architecture*, Wiley-Academy, Chichester, 2006, p.181.

7 Ibid., p.181.

Questions Concerning the Redevelopment of Ground Zero

1 See Deborah Solomon, "Art/Architecture; "From the Rubble,

Ideas for Rebirth", *New York Times*, 30 September, 2001.

2   Ibid.

3   Ibid.

4   See:http://www.lowermanhattan.info/rebuild/timeline/ rebuild_timeline_html_2002.asp#apr – accessed November 2005.

5   Reinhold Martin, "One or More", *Grey Room* 07, Spring 2002, p.116.

6   Ibid., p.116.

7   Ibid.

8   Edward Wyatt, "Longing for a Sept. 10 Skyline; Some Vocal Groups Call for Restoring the Twin Towers", *New York Times*, 2 November, 2002.

9   Here I refer to the Lower Manhattan Development Corporation (LMDC) as a *de facto* arm of government, in as much as it was this body that the State gave *de jure* responsibility to, to conduct the redevelopment (both political and economic) of the lower Manhattan area devastated by the attacks.

10   See Terry Smith's use of the term "iconomy" in "The Political Economy of Iconotypes and the Architecture of Destination: Uluru, The Sydney Opera House and the World Trade Center", *Architectural Theory Review*, Vol. 7 / No. 2, 2002.

11   In the 20 July 2002 Javits Center presentation of the initial master-plan proposals, it was not in fact Beyer Blinder Belle's schemes that were the only ones on view. Accompanying Beyer Blinder Belle's proposals were two proposals by Peterson/Littenberg Architecture and Urban Design, one proposal by Cooper Robertson & Partners, and one further proposal for the site by David Childs/SOM. The presentation of the initial schemes at the Javits Center on 20 July 2002, however, is widely associated with the Beyer Blinder Belle proposals, against which the published and popular criticism arising from the presentations is also

associated with.

12 For the full response of Herbert Muschamp to the initial LMDC proposals presented to the public at the Javits Center see "Visions of Ground Zero: An Appraisal; An Agency's ideology is unsuited to its task", *New York Times*, 17 July 2002.

13 Terry Smith, "The Political Economy of Iconotypes and the Architecture of Destination: Uluru, The Sydney Opera House and the World Trade Center", *Architectural Theory Review*, Vol. 7 / No. 2, 2002, p.1.

14 Ibid.

15 Ibid.

16 New York League of Architects, 2005, After September 11: An Open Meeting, see: www.archleague.org/nyc/nyc.html – site accessed November 2005.

17 Reinhold Martin, "Architecture at War – a report from Ground Zero", in *Angelaki* Vol.9-No.2 August 2004, p.219 and 223.

18 I emphasize the term "responsive" architecture in this instance, which is one of deconstruction and rethinking, as opposed to "progressive" architecture that was the call of *New York Times* architecture critic Herbert Muschamp in response to the redevelopment effort. See: Herbert Muschamp: "Filling The Void: A Chance To Soar", *New York Times*, 30 September, 2001.

19 Reinhold Martin, "Architecture at War – a report from Ground Zero", in *Angelaki* Vol.9-No.2 August 2004 p.224.

20 Ibid., p.224.

21 Ibid., p.219.

22 Ibid., p.224.

23 Gilles Deleuze & Felix. Guattari, *Capitalism and Schizophrenia – A Thousand Plateaus*, The Athlone Press, London, 1996, p.219.

24 Jean-Francois Lyotard: "Rewriting Modernity" in *Sub-stance* 16:3-9, 1987, No.54.

25 Jean-Francois Lyotard, *The Inhuman*, Polity Press, Cambridge, 1991, p.26.

26 I refer here to the deconstructive project in architecture as worked through by Eisenman and others in the 1980s.

27 For the etymological meaning of "pro-" see *Oxford Concise Dictionary of Etymology*, Oxford University Press, Oxford, 1996; with "pro-" representing the combined form of the Greek *pró* before (of time, position, priority).

28 Michel Foucault, "The Subject and Power", in *Art after Modernism: rethinking representation*, The New Museum of Contemporary Art, New York, 1984, p.421.

29 Jean-Francois Lyotard, *Libidinal Economy*, Continuum, London, 1993, p.44.

30 Ibid., p.48.

31 Ibid., p.48.

32 Jean-Francois Lyotard, *Libidinal Economy*, Continuum, London, 1993, p.51.

33 Ibid., p.50.

34 Ibid., p.478.

35 Here it is noteworthy to mention Peter Eisenman's *New York* magazine scheme for Ground Zero in which force-lines are used for the generation of the low-rise elements of the scheme interconnecting his replacement towers. See *Imagining Ground Zero*, Suzanne Stephens (ed.), Thames & Hudson, London, 2004, p.105.

36 Ibid., p.49.

37 Ibid., p.49.

38 Ibid., p.49.

39 Jean Francois Lyotard, *Libidinal Economy*, The Athlone Press, London, 2004, pp.1-40.

40 Gilles Deleuze & Felix Guattari, *A Thousand Plateaus*, The Athlone Press, London, 1996, p.500.

41 Ivan Chtcheglov, "Formulary for a New Urbanism", in Ken Knabb (edited and translated) *Situationist International*

Anthology, Bureau of Public Secrets, Berkeley CA, 1989, p.2.

42   Ibid., p.2.

43   Thomas McDonough, "Fluid Spaces: Constant and the Situationist Critique of Architecture", in Catherine de Zegher and Mark Wigley (eds.), *The Activist Drawing: Retracing Situationist Architectures from Constant's New Babylon to Beyond*, MIT Press, Cambridge MA, 2001, p.95.

44   Ibid., p.131.

45   Ibid., p.478.

46   Ibid., p.97.

47   Iain Borden, "New Babylonians: from the avant-garde to the everyday", in *The Journal of Architecture*, Volume 6, Summer 2001, p.131.

48   Simone Brott, *Architecture for a free Subjectivity – Deleuze and Guattari at the Horizon of the Real*, Ashgate Publishing Limited, Farnham, Surrey, 2011, p.83.

The Possibility for Architecture Theory

1   See *"think"* in the *Oxford Concise Dictionary of English Etymology*, Oxford University Press, Oxford, 1996.

2   Ibid., see "theory"

3   See Introduction, K Michael Hays, *Architecture Theory Since 1968*, MIT Press, Cambridge MA, 1998, p.x.

4   Terry Eagleton, *The Function of Criticism*, Verso, London-New York, 2005, p.90.

5   Ibid., p.90.

6   Ibid., p.90.

7   Ibid., p.x.

8   Ibid., p.x-xi.

9   Ibid., p.xi.

10   Peter Eisenman, *The Formal Basis of Modern Architecture*, Lars Müller Publishers, 2006, p.343.

11   Ibid., p.353.

12   Ibid., p.353.

13 Jane Rendell, et. al. (ed.), *Critical Architecture*, Routledge, Abingdon, 2007, p.2.

14 Ibid., p.2.

15 Ibid., p.1.

16 By "psychoanalytical" it is meant the search for a realization of a new subjectivity, a new way of seeing and perceiving architecture, of thinking about it in a different light.

17 Jane Rendell, et. al. (ed.), *Critical Architecture*, Routledge, Abingdon, 2007, p.1-2.

18 Ibid., p.3.

19 Vincent Descombe, *Modern French Philosophy*, Cambridge University Press, Cambridge, 1980, p.79.

20 Ibid., p.79.

21 Andrew Benjamin, *Architectural Philosophy*, The Athlone Press, London, 2000, p.104.

22 Although Rendell uses the term "criticism" in this quote, I consider criticism to be an outcome and possible extension of theory as stated earlier, something that is derived from and wholly subject to it.

23 Jane Rendell, et. al. (ed.), *Critical Architecture*, Routledge, Abingdon, 2007, p.5.

24 Ibid., p.7.

25 Ben Agger, "Critical Theory, Post-structuralism, Post-modernism: Their Sociological Relevance", *Annual Review of Sociology*, Annual Reviews Inc., 1991, p.124.

26 Quoted from Bernard Tschumi, "Architecture and Transgression", *Oppositions Reader*, Princeton Architectural Press, New York, 1998, p.357.

27 Felix Guattari, "Molecular Revolution and Class Struggle", in *Molecular Revolution*, 1984, p.254.

28 Henri Lefebvre, *The Production of Space*, Blackwell Publishers Ltd., Oxford, 1991, p.419.

29 Ibid., p.419.

On Poetics, *Poiesis* and Architecture

1   Aristotle, *Poetics*, in Introduction by Malcolm Heath, Penguin Books, London, 1996, p. xxviii.
2   Ibid., p. xxviii.
3   Ibid., p. ix.
4   Ibid., p. x.
5   Ibid., p. xiii.
6   Ibid., p. xiv.
7   Ibid., p. xv.
8   Ibid., p. xxxv.
9   Ibid., p. xxxvi.
10 Ibid., p. xvii.
11 Ibid., p. xvii.
12 Ibid., p. xxiii.
13 Ibid., p. xxiii.
14 Ibid., p. xxiv.
15 Ibid., p. xxix.
16 Ibid., p. xxix.
17 Ibid., p. xlix.
18 Ibid., p. xliii.
19 Ibid., p. xxxvii.
20 Ibid., p. xxxviii.
21 Ibid., p. xxxix.
22 Ibid., p. xx.
23 Ibid., p. xxvii.

The Voice of Ruins

1   Christopher Woodward, *In Ruins*, Vintage, London, 2002, p.175.
2   Ibid., p.69.
3   Ibid., p.30.
4   Ibid., p.123.
5   Ibid., p.139.
6   Ibid., p.37.

7   Ibid., p.61.

8   Ibid., p.91.

9   Ibid., p.36.

10 Ibid., p.153.

11 Ibid., p.39.

12 Ibid., p.69.

13 Ibid., p.2-3.

14 Ibid., p.89.

15 Ibid., p.93.

16 Ibid., p.73.

17 Ibid., p.62.

18 From the exhibition text of photographs of Pripyat titled "Chernobyl Nuclear Disaster: 21 years after in photos", by Quintin Lake, held at the Architectural Association, School of Architecture – London, 30 March 2011.

19 Oscar Wilde, *The Picture of Dorian Gray*, Vintage Books, London, 2007, Preface, p.4.

BOOKS

Iff Books is interested in ideas and reasoning. It publishes material on science, philosophy and law. Iff Books aims to work with authors and titles that augment our understanding of the human condition, society and civilisation, and the world or universe in which we live.